D0039412

STRONG MEN

WEAK MEN

From the author's mailbag
in response to *Strong Men, Weak Men*

I do not know when I have been so blessed by a book. I am recommending it to pastors where I go. Your absolute honesty is refreshing. God's strength is made complete in you through your weakness. I pray that the wisdom which flows from your book will help many find the courage to be real.

—B. J. Willhite
The National Prayer Embassy

Your new book is timely and well done. I know several men friends I want to recommend it to. I think I'll suggest it to their wives as a Christmas gift for them.

—Sue Monk Kidd

Strong Men, Weak Men is full of life because it is out of your life.

—Gary Bergel

An extremely timely and meaningful gift. Paul's thorn in the flesh was responsible for teaching him the lesson you're trying to convey—the message of strength discovered in weakness. I guess you and I both have good reason to know what he was talking about!

—Dr. James Dobson

I read your book on men last week and found it an honest and straightforward job, like its creator. It should be helpful to young males groping in the fog that seems to surround so many of them these days.

—Arthur Gordon

I really share your concern about men. Until we get this one solved, I'm not sure that we can get on to the other crises. Males today are confused, frustrated and unsure of their identity.

—Bill Gaither

Very perceptive in many ways.

—Thomas L. Phillips, chairman
Raytheon Corporation

I have been a weak man from a virus for the past couple of weeks, but your words in *Strong Men, Weak Men* brought spiritual strength, for which I am deeply grateful.

—*Fulton Oursler, Jr., editor-in-chief*
Guideposts

Your book should speak to us all.

—*Pat Robertson*

Well written, well-thought-out and most certainly timely. It's a long overdue book.

—*John Sherrill*

Enjoyed it immensely.

—*Richard Armstrong, professor emeritus*
Princeton Theological Seminary

I so appreciate your book that I am passing it around to my Wednesday morning Bible study of some forty men. Strength does come out of weakness.

—*John Erickson, director*
Basketball Operations,
The Big Eight Conference

A timely book. My wife, who is a family life therapist, is taking a look at it as a tool in her counseling.

—*Cal Thomas*
Los Angeles Times Syndicate

The Holy Spirit has led me to use it as a guide in upcoming discussions in our men's breakfast meetings.

—*Rev. Robert Walton, pastor*
Community Bible Chapel
Barre, Vermont

Wonderful! You are scratching where a lot of people are itching!

—*Dr. O. S. Hawkins, pastor*
First Baptist Church
Dallas, Texas

STRONG MEN
WEAK MEN

LEONARD E. LeSOURD

Chosen Books
A Division of Baker Book House Co
Grand Rapids, Michigan 49516

© 1990 by Leonard E. LeSourd

Published by Chosen Books
a division of Baker Book House Company
P.O. Box 6287, Grand Rapids, MI 49516-6287

Printed in the United States of America

All rights reserved. No part of this publication may be reproduced, stored in a
retrieval system, or transmitted in any form or by any means—electronic,
mechanical, photocopy, recording, or any other—without the prior written permission of the publisher. The only exception is brief quotations in printed
reviews.

First paperback edition 1994.

Library of Congress Cataloging-in-Publication Data

LeSourd, Leonard E.
    Strong men, weak men / Leonard E. LeSourd
        p. cm.
    ISBN 0-8007-9211-4
    1. Men—Religious life.   2. Men (Christian theology)   3. Men—
    United States. I. Title.
    BV4843.L47   1990
    248.8'42—dc20   90-35761

Scripture quotations identified KJV are from the King James Version of the Bible.

Scripture quotations identified NKJ are from The New King James Version.
Copyright © 1979, 1980, 1982, Thomas Nelson, Inc., Publishers.

Scripture quotations identified LB are taken from *The Living Bible,* copyright ©
1971 by Tyndale House Publishers, Wheaton, Illinois. Used by permission.

Scripture quotations identified NAS are from the New American Standard Bible,
© the Lockman Foundation 1960, 1962, 1963, 1968, 1971, 1972, 1973, 1975, 1977.

Scripture quotations identified NIV are from the HOLY BIBLE, NEW INTER-
NATIONAL VERSION®. NIV®. Copyright © 1973, 1978, 1984 by International
Bible Society. Used by permission of Zondervan Publishing House. All rights
reserved.

Scripture quotations identified TEV are from the *Good News Bible*—Old Testament: Copyright © American Bible Society 1976; New Testament: Copyright ©
American Bible Society 1966, 1971, 1976.

STRONG MEN WEAK MEN

LEONARD E. LeSOURD

Chosen Books

A Division of Baker Book House Co
Grand Rapids, Michigan 49516

© 1990 by Leonard E. LeSourd

Published by Chosen Books
a division of Baker Book House Company
P.O. Box 6287, Grand Rapids, MI 49516-6287

Printed in the United States of America

All rights reserved. No part of this publication may be reproduced, stored in a retrieval system, or transmitted in any form or by any means—electronic, mechanical, photocopy, recording, or any other—without the prior written permission of the publisher. The only exception is brief quotations in printed reviews.

First paperback edition 1994.

Library of Congress Cataloging-in-Publication Data

LeSourd, Leonard E.
    Strong men, weak men / Leonard E. LeSourd
       p. cm.
    ISBN 0-8007-9211-4
    1. Men—Religious life.   2. Men (Christian theology)   3. Men—
    United States. I. Title.
    BV4843.L47   1990
    248.8'42—dc20   90-35761

Scripture quotations identified KJV are from the King James Version of the Bible.

Scripture quotations identified NKJ are from The New King James Version. Copyright © 1979, 1980, 1982, Thomas Nelson, Inc., Publishers.

Scripture quotations identified LB are taken from *The Living Bible*, copyright © 1971 by Tyndale House Publishers, Wheaton, Illinois. Used by permission.

Scripture quotations identified NAS are from the New American Standard Bible, © the Lockman Foundation 1960, 1962, 1963, 1968, 1971, 1972, 1973, 1975, 1977.

Scripture quotations identified NIV are from the HOLY BIBLE, NEW INTERNATIONAL VERSION®. NIV®. Copyright © 1973, 1978, 1984 by International Bible Society. Used by permission of Zondervan Publishing House. All rights reserved.

Scripture quotations identified TEV are from the *Good News Bible*—Old Testament: Copyright © American Bible Society 1976; New Testament: Copyright © American Bible Society 1966, 1971, 1976.

TO

My father, Howard Marion LeSourd,
a strong-weak man in the highest sense.

WITH GRATITUDE . . .

To Yvonne Burgan for her artistry with the computer, her flair for research, and her patience with my endless changes; to Elaine Brink for her secretarial skills and practical suggestions; to Theresa Mulligan for her scriptural expertise.

To Elizabeth (Tib) Sherrill for her creative ideas (where did she learn so much about men?) and her incomparable editing assistance.

To my children, Linda, Chet and Jeff, who contributed much to this book and who make this father proud to be a father.

To my wife, Sandy, whose caring heart and joyful spirit won every member of our family and who has that special gift of knowing how to spark a man to feel like a man.

Contents

Introduction

"The man of the '90s is a man under a microscope."

The *USA Today* report goes on to state that today's men are confused, frustrated, unsure of themselves in comparison to men eventhirty years ago.

Are men weaker today in the wake of the women's movement? "I believe so," says Alvin Baraff, founder in 1984 of the Men-Center in Washington, D.C. "Women have been marching along now for twenty to thirty years, and we men have been standing by and watching the parade and not jumping in."

But is this the kind of parade men want to join? Most men would say no.

In his book *Healing the Masculine Soul* Gordon Dalbey states that "men do not know who they are as men. They tend to define themselves by what they do, who they know, or what they own."

But does this represent a change—a decline of

strength—or have most men always been weak, with only a few across the centuries demonstrating real leadership and character? Perhaps men's weaknesses are simply more visible today.

It was in 1975 that I began collecting research on the changing roles and self-perception of men. The accumulated evidence of fifteen years is disturbing, and at the same time filled with promise.

Disturbing indeed are the high-profile issues . . . men in government forced to resign because of unethical conduct . . . church leaders convicted of sexual crimes . . . pornography and adultery eating away men's integrity, destroying marriages. Nothing new about any of this, of course, except perhaps our decreasing capacity for shock and outrage.

Man's confusion is what's new—his loss of identity, his frustration over what he sees as a switch in basic assumptions.

He may blame women for this dilemma, as did Marc Lepine who on December 6, 1989, in a fit of rage put on his hunting gear, grabbed his rifle and stormed into the University of Montreal Engineering School, shouting, "You're all a bunch of feminists." He shot at random, killing fourteen women and wounding twelve others.

Tragedies like this when men go berserk—and there have been too many of them in recent years—reveal the need for more study and research into why men are what they are and do what they do. And that's the promising side of the picture: Malaise is leading to an increased self-awareness on the part of men, a new readiness to probe beneath surface living, a rejection of unexamined stereotypes.

In 1982 Eugene August, a professor at Ohio University at Dayton, began teaching the course "Modern Men: Images and Reality." It was a lonely specialty at first. "Today the number of serious studies of men has mushroomed on campuses across the nation," August states.

An interesting sidelight: Women are showing themselves more interested in these courses than men; seventy percent of men's studies students are females.

Obviously women are as baffled as men over the contradictions and inconsistencies of male behavior—and more willing, at present, than men to work at relationships.

Hobart College in upstate New York held a month-long conference on "Men and Masculinity" early in 1990 for the fifth straight year. Objective—to probe the mysteries of manhood.

Fuller Theological Seminary has a new course, "Men in Difficult Times," the purpose of which is to produce a new agenda for Christian men.

Edwin Louis Cole, president of Manhood, Inc., holds seminars and conferences worldwide in which he challenges men to a new boldness in the 1990s to make these years "A Decade of Daring."

"*Real* men's studies is just in the embryonic stages," says Warren Farrell, author of *Why Men Are the Way They Are*. "The major media are just becoming receptive to studies which present the men's side of the story as well as the women's."

Along with tracing these first stirrings of the "men's movement," I've looked back over the years of my own life. Three marriages. The first, to Eve, ended in divorce—a major failure. Yet out of it came three wonderful children and many fine memories. A second and fulfilling marriage of 23 years to Catherine, an extraordinary woman of literary talent, was ended by her death in 1983. My current marriage, since 1985, is to Sandy, another remarkable woman with a ministry to hurting people. She is teaching me a lot about joy and how to smell the flowers.

Many years, many roles. Grandfather now to seven! Stepfather, first to Catherine's son, now also to Sandy's three children. Father-in-law to two strong women. Strong women, in fact, are the norm in our family.

From boyhood I seem to have found my identity in the roles I filled. In World War II, I spent three and a half years as an Air Corps pilot, training air cadets to fly in combat. Since 1946, my job description has been "religious publisher." First as the editor of *Guideposts* magazine for 28 years, then publisher and part-owner of Chosen Books Publishing Company. During that time, I have written, rewritten, edited or shepherded into publication some 2,500 articles and more than 100 books—many of them by, with or about men. In the process I have found some answers to the issues facing men today—and an almost equal number of questions.

Perhaps the most disturbing one is: Why hasn't the Christian faith spoken more clearly to these issues? Men professing a belief in Christ seem to be almost as confused, frustrated and unsure of their identities as those who do not. Recent figures on divorce, for example, show that 51 percent of non-Christian marriages end in divorce; 46 percent of Christian ones.

Strong Men, Weak Men is written out of my own struggle for men who, like me, believe in God, but are seeking answers as to why they are in this world and what is

We all know a few strong men, creative men, dynamic men, courageous men, fulfilled men. Trouble is, there should be more, so many more.

The good news and hope of the world is that a change is under way. It has begun in the academic world, been seized on by businesses, explored by men's groups meeting in an ever-increasing number of offices, churches, homes. Men everywhere are coming together to rediscover and redefine their masculinity. Men's organizations are springing up all over the world to re-ignite the fire that sent a small band of Christ's disciples into a pagan world with the boldness of a new vision.

The survival of this planet will depend on how males in the months and years ahead respond to the challenge to become strong men.

Strong women will be an essential part of the process, but strong women alone will not heal and restore our sick world.

As I see it, men have a mandate from God that we cannot and must not abdicate—to be healers of the world's misery, bearers of His standard, heralds of His Word.

Leonard E. LeSourd
Evergreen Farm
April 19, 1990

required of them as men. It focuses on what the Wor
God is saying to us as single men, as sons, as husbar
brothers, bosses and all the other roles assigned to us
changing world.

Some of the individuals I have had in mind as I write
as follows:

- A deeply religious husband and father, married to a highly successful businesswoman,
  who is concerned over his family role.
- A recently divorced man, defeated in marriage,
  who wants to dedicate his life to God, but feels
  condemned by the churchgoing people he
  knows.
- An overachieving male, professionally at the
  top of his field, but inwardly restless and spiritually dead, who yearns for something beyond himself.
- A Washington politician, weary of unethical
  behavior, who seeks a moral basis upon which
  to build his public career.
- A predatory single male who is sick of his lifestyle and confessed to Sandy and me that what
  he really longs for is a pure wife and a holy life.
- A churchman who doesn't know how to relate
  to women in leadership.
- And a number of women in our own church
  who recently asked our group of elders for help
  in understanding the troubled men in their
  lives.

Are Men an Endangered Species?

Here are some statistics:
Population in USA (1990 U.S. Census estimate):*
Men   121,000,000
Women   127,000,000
The ratio of men's to women's deaths today:
Lung cancer—men 6 to 1 over women
Other bronchopulmonic diseases—men 5 to 1
Suicides—men 2.7 to 1
Heart disease—men 2 to 1
Auto accidents—men 2.5 to 1
Other statistics:
People in prison (1988):
Men 573,990,   women 30,834
Diagnosed cases of AIDS (1988):
Men 68,306,   women 6,260
Homeless (HUD estimate 1989):
Single men—165,000 to 231,000
Single women—32,000 to 45,000

American Health, January–February 1989

*Encouraging news for men: In April 1990 the Census Bureau reported that during the 1980s the number of men grew faster than the number of women by about 100,000—the first such increase since 1900–1910. Reason: fewer cancer deaths among men.

STRONG
MEN
WEAK
MEN

1
The Macho Myth

Thou shalt have no other gods before me.

Exodus 20:3, KJV

It was in the late 1960s that I first became aware of the difference. I was talking to a group of men and women on a subject I was deeply concerned about.

As I spoke, I was searching out responsive faces. In the second row was a woman with a blue dress and dark hair. Her face was alive with interest. Near her another woman, hair almost white, was equally receptive, eyes glowing. There was another, four rows back: Quick understanding leaped between us—a true spirit-to-spirit silent communication.

The men, on the other hand, had faces blank of expression. Here and there a flicker of emotion, but nothing like the women. By the time I had finished my talk, I was convinced that I had somehow turned off or simply bored the men.

Afterward, though, came a surprise. More men than women approached me with questions and comments.

Some of the most frozen-faced males showed the greatest interest.

As the years passed, I became accustomed, as a speaker, to this difference between the sexes. There were exceptions, of course, but about nine out of ten people with responsive faces in an audience were women.

Why is this? Why this dichotomy in men between mind and emotion—or at any rate the expression of emotion? Was it always this way? Have we always had trouble lining up our heads with our hearts? Or is something new and strange happening to men?

Soon after World War II began Jonathan Daniels, President Roosevelt's administrative assistant, proclaimed: "America has become magnificently male again. The twenties are gone with self-indulgence, the thirties with their self-pity. The forties are here with Americans standing on the continent as men . . . fighting in the crudest man terms."

Man terms—does the club, the spear, the bomb, define the male?

Victorious in battle against a powerful foe, we American men returned from World War II with a palpable sense of our power, leadership and position in life. We were saviors of freedom. We had shown valor and fortitude and competence. We were overcomers. America emerged from World War II as the unquestioned leader of the world.

For those of us in the Air Corps one development had briefly threatened our male dominance. A women's flying unit was formed (WAF) and there were occasions when female pilots joined their male counterparts in ferrying single-engine planes from one base to another. The women handled the aircraft as well as the men. Then a story circulated to reassure us. Women could fly the planes O.K., but in an emergency when they instituted bailout procedures, their relatively weaker muscle strength was a fatal handicap and they went down with the plane. So with some relief we concluded that we had to be protective of the WAFs, Lord bless them.

After the war men returned to their jobs, many of which had been held by women. Though women surrendered their positions to the returning heroes, they had proven themselves in the workplace.

So in the late 1940s, it was still a man's world. That blunt phrase *male chauvinism* had yet to appear; able women still tried to hide the fact of their competence. Sure, there were arrogance and abusiveness and hardheartedness on the part of many males, but wasn't that always true of the victors? And of men through the ages?

Macho Champions

The macho male had a great champion in General George S. Patton, "Old Blood and Guts," as he was called by his fighting men. He freely admitted he loved war, when "men were men." In battle he was a brilliant leader.

The movie *Patton* captured the general's macho spirit on film. Who can forget the opening scene when George C. Scott, who played Patton, strode on stage in front of an enormous American flag, dressed in full military regalia: combat helmet, chest full of medals, pearl-handled revolver, knee-high boots, riding whip in hand?

"All real Americans love to fight," he announced. "American men love the sting of battle. When you were kids, your heroes were athletes, men in action. You love a

u won't tolerate a loser. The thought of losing

ourse this winner's mentality was an incomparable asset on the battlefield, as his tank division drove
ahead of all others into the heart of Germany, or as he led
exhausted troops for days without sleep to rescue trapped
Allied forces in the Battle of the Bulge.

Ernest Hemingway was another whose lifestyle captured the imagination of males during the postwar period.
Hemingway's enthusiasms included boxing, bullfighting,
big game hunting and, of course, drinking. Such books as
A Farewell to Arms and *For Whom the Bell Tolls* made men
yearn for a life of adventure.

More recently Pete Rose, the ultimate All-Star ballplay-
er, gave a new generation of boys an image of no-holds-
barred masculinity. Pete made more base hits (4,256) than
anyone else ever has, or probably ever will. Called "Charlie Hustle," he would run to first base when given a walk,
and once plowed so hard into an opposing catcher during
an All-Star game that he dislocated the man's shoulder.
Rose gave all of himself to the game and the fans loved
him for it.

Strong men, courageous men, macho men . . . they
were role models for millions.

Boys Don't Cry

My own entry into the world of machismo occurred on
a Saturday afternoon when I was twelve years old. Three
of us boys entered the local movie theatre in Newton,
Massachusetts, and took seats in the fifth row. The film

featured a lovable collie who at the story's climax rescued a small boy from a pond, at the cost of his own life.

As the dog's limp body was pulled from the water I sobbed uncontrollably. Then came self-consciousness and an agonizing sense of embarrassment. *Everybody must be looking at me!*

You are a baby to cry this way! I lashed out at myself. Sternly I pulled myself together: *Boys don't cry . . . boys don't cry.*

As we walked from the theatre I issued an irrevocable order: *You are never to cry again!*

From that day on I would sit tensely in motion picture theatres, bracing to resist any sad scenes. *This is all make-believe,* I'd intone. *The director sits there . . . the camera is up there. . . .* I had begun the process of anesthetizing myself not to feel emotions.

This self-imposed training gained new urgency in the Air Corps. While at Radio Operators School at Scott Field, Illinois, I happened to see a film showing pilots preening about in their uniforms, being irresistible to every woman they encountered. Impressed more by this, I think, than any basic desire to conquer a new skill, I applied for transfer to pilot school, completed single-engine training in July 1943 and asked for overseas combat. Instead, I was assigned to Randolph Field, San Antonio, Texas, to become a flying instructor, which I did for the balance of the war.

Now I was faced with situations that could not be dismissed as "make-believe." I had some narrow escapes while teaching night flying and a lot of stress in a stepped-up training program that sent pilots overseas with inadequate instruction. One after another, close flying buddies were killed in training accidents. To defend myself from "unmanly" emotions, I developed a philosophy of living for the moment: eat, drink and be merry—the classic escapes from unpleasant reality.

Once at a good-bye party for a woman flying instructor we all loved, I saw with dismay that she was beginning to cry. Feeling my tears about to surface, too, I fled the scene. This wasn't strength, of course, but cowardice, but my efforts to model myself after the macho heroes of the day prevented my seeing this.

On dates I learned to play it light and easy; feint with a serious statement, then turn it into a little joke on myself. Underplay my flying escapades: "There I was upsidedown at ten thousand feet when the damnedest thing happened. . . ." The story that followed might or might not be true. It didn't much matter as long as it ended in a laugh on myself. The worst offense of all was to take life too seriously.

Then near the end of the war I met The Girl. Mary Jane was articulate, perceptive, daughter of a prominent Texas family. One day as we were driving from San Antonio to her father's ranch, Mary Jane queried me about my life as a pilot. "Do you have any fears?"

"Yes, but I don't dwell on them."

"Any special one?"

"Death."

"How do you deal with it?"

I was silent for a while, struggling between my inclination to demonstrate imperturbability and a sudden desire to be honest. Sensing that Mary Jane would see through any deception, I decided to level with her.

"I pretend indifference."

She looked at me quickly. "Why the pretense?"

"Pilots are supposed to be cool, unflappable."

"So you pretend to be what you're not."

"No, I become what I pretend to be."

She paused to digest this, then continued, "Are any pilots honest about their fears?"

"If so, they probably washed out in training."

"So indifference is your credo for life, Len?"

"I prefer the word *nonchalance*. We pilots aren't indifferent to life. I don't feel indifferent to you, Mary Jane."

Mary Jane was silent as we entered a village where she guided her small car through a series of quick turns. Her soft auburn hair was loose on her shoulders. I reached over and ran my fingers through one curl.

"Do you have a goal in life, Len?"

"To live through the war," I replied with a smile.

Mary Jane didn't smile back. She was usually responsive to banter, but not now.

"When the war is over I'd like to write a novel," I added. "I'll buy myself a car, put everything I own in the trunk and tour the country."

"What will you write about?"

"Pilots. How they adjust to civilian life."

"Do you think pilots will have a harder time adjusting than, say, combat troops?"

"Good question. Pilots don't usually see the people they kill; they won't have those kinds of memories to deal with. Yet pilots have a steady dose of excitement. They fly high, they live high. It'll be hard to find all that in civilian life."

"What will your novel say?"

I couldn't really answer that question. The uncomfortable truth was I had little to say. I could invent a plot and build a love story, but that was it. My philosophy of nonchalance was already beginning to dry me up on the inside. I didn't realize any of this at the time, and for the rest of that day kept up my efforts to impress Mary Jane. But my shallowness had shown through.

I courted Mary Jane with all my artfulness and persistence. She seemed to like me, but my guess is she had a different label for me than *nonchalant*. Was it *lightweight*?

I didn't see her during a month's special assignment away from Texas. When I returned a letter was awaiting me. She had become engaged to an old friend. On the outside I shrugged it off. Inside I knew she was a very special woman and I was the loser.

The Frozen Male

The Air Corps abounded in macho males. I flew with them, played poker with them, drank with them, emulated them. Swearing was an art form with us; four-letter words became nouns, adjectives, verbs, adverbs. Nicknames were the rule. In the course of a raucous singing episode at the officers' club late one night, my rendition of a blues song earned me the label *Torchy*. It follows me to this day.

None of us realized, at the time, that in acquiring this sought-after macho exterior, we were losing something far more important. We were losing touch with our own inner reality. Our feelings became shockproof. We wore hard, protective crusts about our true selves like shields. We became "frozen males."

How would I describe myself on my discharge in late 1945? A completely self-centered single male. Self-gratification was the beginning and the end. The sex drive was dominant, of course, but self-centeredness makes other demands—sleep, food, drink, approval, applause. Seeds had been planted in me and many others to make us inflexible husbands, weak fathers, unemotional lovers, rigid leaders.

What I wasn't ready to face up to was my deadness of spirit. The philosophy of nonchalance may have helped me cope with fear, but it was death to conscience and idealism. The "I don't care" approach can't be assigned to just a certain segment of experience. It seeps into every phase of your life, numbing your responses to people. Others sense you don't care about them, and give back the same to you.

I cared about Mary Jane, but realize looking back that I had been unwilling to open up, be vulnerable, risk rejection. Mary Jane never found out who the real Len LeSourd was. I wasn't sure who he was either.

The word *macho* is defined as "a strong or exaggerated sense of power or the right to dominate . . . assertive manliness." To instill this manliness, the majority of boys growing up in the 1930s, '40s and '50s were put through a conditioning process at home, in school, in the community. The pattern is still depressingly familiar. A boy discovers he likes birds or music, but is pulled away from such interests to engage in sports he does not like at all. He cries when his dog dies and is told tears are not manly. He puts his arm affectionately around his good friend only to be admonished sternly that "boys don't hug other boys." If he plays too much with girls, he is called a sissy.

Later on, if the teenager does not go out with girls, he is called queer. If he is honest about his shortcomings, he will be rebuked and told a man covers up such things. By

29

the time he reaches manhood many of the genuine discoveries he's made about himself have been discarded on the advice of family and friends. In place of the real self is a plastic person molded and shaped to "make it" in the hard tough world.

These are the men who remain frozen-faced while listening to an impassioned speech. Hardly a muscle twitches in their faces when confronted with a setback in business or the death of a friend. They pride themselves on bearing pain stoically, not realizing that humanity and creativity have been drained out of them. In T. S. Eliot's famous lines about "the hollow man" and "the stuffed men" they are:

> Leaning together
> Headpiece filled with straw. Alas!

Man in the Iron Mask

The Richard Nixon administration produced some famous stone-faced males, including Chuck Colson, the "hatchet man," and G. Gordon Liddy, the "Man in the Iron Mask." If there were an award for macho behavior in the last twenty years it would surely go to Liddy, who titled his autobiography simply *Will.*

"I became what I wanted to be," Liddy states.

Behind those words is a case study in machismo.

Fear dominated Liddy's early life. He was small and would run blocks out of his way home to avoid the bigger boys.

The change began after a Sunday Mass. "Human beings

are created in the image and likeness of God," the priest had said.

God does not fear, young Liddy told himself. To remake himself in this fearless image, "I knew what I had to do," Liddy recalls, "and I dreaded it. To change myself from a puny, fearful boy to a strong, fearless man, I would have to face my fears, one by one, and overcome them."

And face them he did. A fear of heights was overcome by climbing to the roof of his New Jersey apartment and leaping from rooftop to rooftop when a slip would mean a seven-story plunge to certain death.

He took the same head-on approach to the huge wharf rats that terrorized him along the Hudson River docks. One day he faced an especially large one at the end of a wharf. "Never corner a rat," he had been told. Liddy was backing away when remorse at his cowardice over-whelmed him. "The shame of it brought tears to my eyes," he wrote. "I stopped, then advanced upon the rat who suddenly jumped into the water and swam away."

"You yellow rat!" Liddy shouted triumphantly. It was the first live enemy he had vanquished.

Bigger boys were next. Liddy took a course in karate. Defeats followed, but Liddy came back for more. Soon the bullies avoided him.

By college his frontal-attack style was perfected. Liddy acquired a degree in law, had a stint with the FBI, then an appointment to the Treasury Department before being asked to join the White House staff.

Aware that Nixon admired macho types, Liddy set out to outmacho them all. Then came Watergate. Liddy's con-frontational philosophy disrupted the court proceedings and infuriated Judge Sirica who sentenced Liddy to twenty years, far in excess of the other sentences. Civil suits totaling millions were leveled against him.

But Liddy never stopped attacking. In the end he served only a little more than four years and at the conclusion of the litigation, "I lost not one cent and had a hell of a lot of fun," he claims.

On the surface Liddy's autobiography chronicles a success story. But let's look closer. The book does not disclose the cost of his combative lifestyle to his wife and five children. Except for one revealing episode. After four years in prison, Liddy is freed. His loving wife, Fran, is there to meet him in the family car. So, too, are a host of reporters.

What does Liddy do? Brushing off his wife's protests, he jumps into the driver's seat and roars off, the reporters in three cars in frantic pursuit.

The macho Liddy is in full charge. In a wild "cops and robbers" chase scene, he drives at high speed in and out of traffic, going the wrong way down a one-way street, tying up traffic, terrorizing pedestrians and turning his wife into a sobbing, traumatized, limp figure beside him.

Yes, Liddy loses the pursuing reporters . . . and probably a host of readers, too, who up to this point in the book may have been admirers.

The fatal flaw in the macho personality is exposed near the end of the book. Liddy takes the Danbury prison officials to court for violations of prison rules; he prosecutes the case himself against a lawyer from the Bureau of Prisons and top prison officials including the warden himself—*and wins!*

When Liddy appears afterward in the prison yard, inmates spring to their feet, raising their fists in salute, shouting, cheering. "A feeling of immense power came over me . . . my right arm shot out, palm down and was answered by a roar of approval," Liddy writes. "In that moment I felt like a god."

Gordon Liddy did indeed achieve an impressive victory over childhood fears and weakness. But the result was to make him *feel like a god.*

The Fall of the Gods

This is the true bottom line for all of us seduced by the macho myth. Most won't admit it, least of all to ourselves, but the ultimate goal is to prove ourselves godlike. And this, of course, is a monstrous ego trip, which inevitably leads to a fall, to defeat and in many cases to destruction.

What about General George Patton, the great hero of World War II? His fall began when he encountered a weeping soldier in a hospital behind the front lines. Patton became enraged, slapped and kicked him, called him "a yellow-bellied coward" and ordered him back to his unit. When the incident received worldwide publicity, Patton was for a while relieved of his command. Later, at the end of the war, Patton's ego and shoot-from-the-hip approach to Russia convinced the top brass that he was unfit for peacetime service, and he was forced into retirement.

A sad ending, too, for Ernest Hemingway. For most of his life he did indeed loom godlike, larger than life. "The trouble is," wrote Hemingway's biographer, A. E. Hotchner, "when a man is labeled macho, he tries to live up to it. This can be a real trap." It was a trap for Hemingway. It made him incapable of fidelity; he was married four times. He used alcohol to avoid admitting to painful personal situations. At the approach of old age, rather than face the diminishment and loss of power common to humankind, he shot himself in the mouth, leaving his brains on the wall for his wife to clean up.

Especially disillusioning, the Pete Rose situation. Here is a man who seemingly had it all: extraordinary achievements, hero worship from young and old, a top job as manager of the Cincinnati Reds following his retirement. But his ego was so monumental that he once made a scene in a Manhattan restaurant because there was no sandwich named after him. He became a gambling addict, feeling so godlike that when he bet on games involving his own team, a serious offense punishable by banishment from baseball, he felt somehow immune. When the blow fell and Rose was expelled from the game for life, he seemed dazed, hardly comprehending that he had done anything wrong.

Throughout history how many men have been seduced by the illusion that man can fill the role of God? King David, Solomon, Caesar, Napoleon, Hitler, Stalin, Mao . . . the folly persists. The macho ideal can produce men who excel in sports and in war, but their strength is one-dimensional. When they face other tests of manhood—becoming a respected husband, a good father, a moral leader—they often fail.

So we confront a question: If macho males are not the strong men of today, who are? Is there a breed of males, little known, who meet the full-dimensional test of real men, strong men?

Questions for Reflection

1) What is your definition of a strong man?
2) Can you name others in Scripture or world

history who were destroyed when they tried
to live as gods?

3) Are there sects or groups today teaching that
anyone can become godlike?

4) What should be the Christlike approach today
to those with big egos?

5) If you know you have an enlarged ego, how
are you dealing with it?

2
Single Male

God wants you to be holy and pure.

1 Thessalonians 4:3, LB

"The statistics are overwhelming," writes George Gilder in his book *Naked Nomads*. "The single man tends to move from one sexual partner to another, from job to job, city to city, rotating his life without growth or progress. . . . In a sense the bachelor may never grow up."

Indeed the statistics about single males paint a strange and alarming picture:

- Single males earn only half as much as married men.
- They have far more psychological problems than married men and single women.
- They are more than three times as likely to have a nervous breakdown as single women.
- Though single men over age 14 number about 13 percent of the population, they make up 60

percent of the criminals and commit 90 percent of major and violent crimes.

- They account for the vast majority of homeless.
- Because so many live chaotic, rudderless lives, they are considered poor risks by banks and insurance companies.

Most depressing of all for young single men are the statistics on death. Their suicides come four times as often as single women's, four times as often as young married men's. Their overall death rate is so much higher than any other group that it defies actuarial logic. (And these statistics compiled in the 1970s do not include deaths from AIDS.)

Why this dismal track record for the unmarried man—so at odds with the popular stereotype of the fun-loving and carefree bachelor? Far from the unencumbered playboy of fiction, the actual portrait more often reveals a confused and unsuccessful human being, insecure and immature.

I can relate to this statistical profile. I was a single male until age 29, rootless, faithless, purposeless.

How did I get that way?

Some Never Grow Up

I've thought back to the years of my bachelorhood, looking for clues, and have come up with a small but revealing episode. It happened when I was a sophomore at Ohio Wesleyan University. I fell hard for a vivacious blonde.

37

Carol was not only beautiful, but had an aloof queenliness.

I took her on expensive dates. I sent her flowers and candy. It was an all-out expression of my admiration, and a miserable flop. There came a time when she was always dated up whenever I called her.

The real blow came some weeks later. While working on the college yearbook one afternoon, I found myself next to a fellow editor, known for her bluntness. She asked me, "Do you still like Carol?"

I shrugged, suddenly wary.

"I wouldn't waste any time on her," the girl continued. "Why?"

"Well, you might as well know the truth. She says you were too nice to her."

"I was what?"

"Too nice. She says nice guys are boring."

I was stunned. Feelings of embarrassment soon turned to rage—not at Carol, but at my own vulnerability. *You stupid, dumb, mindless fool!* I berated myself.

The anger passed with time, of course, but the residue was a deep feeling of hurt, a sense of being betrayed by the female sex in general. I had been open in my affection, and Carol had not only been turned off by it, she had held me up to ridicule. Instead of seeing Carol as a self-centered young woman with her own problems, I concluded that I was the one who needed to change. "Never again," I vowed, "will I be my natural self around women."

The experience reinforced the vow I'd taken at age twelve never to cry again. To avoid being hurt, build a wall around your emotional life. Anesthetize yourself in various ways (alcohol was one). Develop the art of gamesmanship in your relationship with women. Hurt before you get hurt.

When I was graduated from Ohio Wesleyan in 1941, I was well on my way to becoming the kind of bachelor who never grew up, the kind insurance companies are so wary of. Two of my college friends and I rented an apartment in Greenwich Village, New York City. Three bachelors living together in such a setting can generate a lot of activity. The invitation we worked out for our housewarming party went like this:

> We invite you to spar
> At our homemade bar.
> It's not very far
> By subway or car.
>
> > Dave, Ken and Len
> > One Christopher Street

It seems unbelievable now, but my income of $32.50 a week covered rent, clothes, food, gas, garage and maintenance for my car, bottled entertainment and an occasional sortie with a date to the Cafe Rouge at the Pennsylvania Hotel. Breakfast was ten cents (the Nedick special: coffee, orange juice, one doughnut), lunch thirty cents (soup and a sandwich), and dinner something we whipped up in the apartment. Travel to work was a nickel each way on the subway.

I worked hard at my job in a public relations firm, but lived for the New York night life. It was fun to shock our friends from Ohio by taking them to the Howdy Club, where transvestites, lesbians and gays mingled together. Remember, this was 1941.

At the time I thought all this was truly the good life. There were few responsibilities, lots of parties, many casual friends. When I left the city in June 1942 to join the Army, I fitted perfectly the description the late Sam Shoemaker had for all those genial people who have no purpose in life. He called them "amiable nonentities."

In the Air Corps it didn't take me long to fit into the mold of the "hot pilot." First I took the grommet out of my officer's visored cap so that the sides would dip in, and learned to tilt it at the proper angle. I wore my dark brown sunglasses everywhere, sometimes even at night. The look on my face had the proper blend of coolness, roguishness and arrogance, depending on whether I was trying to impress males or females.

As flying instructors we were encouraged to take weekend flights to other bases in the U.S. On one weekend seared in my memory, three of us flew separate single-engine planes to Dallas, Texas, from our base in Coffeyville, Kansas. We arrived in Dallas early Saturday, giving us an afternoon and evening for fun. Sunday morning would be "sleep-it-off" time before we flew back to Kansas Sunday afternoon.

On this particular weekend, my two buddies were Chuck and Tom, both convivial single types. Saturday night was always party night and you never had to leave the hotel to find one. Our strategy: Pick any floor, get off the elevator, listen and go in the direction of the noise. The Air Corps pilot's uniform was our badge of admission. I can still see Chuck's wide grin and hear his

"Howdy, friends" as he moved into a happy throng of total strangers.

The next morning Chuck was still in a party mood as we thumbed through the Sunday papers.

"Let's order some beer," he suggested.

Alcohol before a flight was a standard no-no. Tom and I just frowned at him.

"Look outside. It's a beautiful day. The flight to Kansas is a piece of cake," Chuck persisted.

"How do you know what the weather is in Kansas?" I asked.

"A little birdie told me that the visibility there is unlimited."

When Tom and I still shook our heads, Chuck snorted, picked up the phone and ordered three bottles of ale. Chuck's thirst was obvious, and I was tempted to drink one bottle to keep him from guzzling all three. But I didn't—and he did.

When we got to the airport in the middle of the afternoon, Chuck seemed steady enough, yet I felt uneasy. Even a small amount of alcohol in the blood can lessen judgment. If hazardous weather confronts a pilot, the slightest dizziness can turn into vertigo—and the weather report for Kansas was not reassuring. A front was moving in: We'd be lucky to make it to Coffeyville before the bad weather arrived.

We took off one after the other. Half an hour from the Coffeyville Air Base, I ran into heavy clouds. These, plus oncoming darkness, made the approach and landing a tense experience. Tom and I taxied up to the ramp almost together. We waited in Operations for Chuck. He never arrived.

The next day they found his plane and his body in a cornfield forty miles west of the airport. There seemed to be no explanation for the crash. Tom and I knew differently.

Set Your Trim Tabs

There's a lot about those bachelor years between 1943 and 1948 that I would like to forget. Yet they help me understand how early, all-but-unconscious decisions can shape a lifetime course.

In the training planes I flew then was a set of controls called *trim tabs*. When the plane reached the desired altitude, I adjusted my trim tabs so that the plane would fly straight ahead even with my hands off the stick.

In the same way, a young man, almost without knowing it, can put the direction of his life on automatic. The set of his will, like the trim tabs, can steer him to church on a Sunday morning, or to the golf course, or to sleep the morning away. It determines whom he seeks out as friends, what they do together—in short, the use he makes of his status as a single male.

Many set their course toward self-indulgence. I did. But there are at least two other directions open to young unmarried men. I wish I had seen this more clearly. I wish the books, magazines, films of the '40s and '50s had portrayed these other lifestyles as energetically as they did the irresponsible "glamour boy." As I see it, the bachelor can head in one of three directions:

1. *Self-Centered Singleness.* The man traveling this road seeks pleasure, possessions, adulation. Since his world revolves around himself, he is tempted by drugs, pornog-

raphy, crime. Those who travel this path are in danger of becoming gloomy bachelor statistics.

2. *Toward Marriage.* Males taking this course see marriage as an undertaking every bit as important as a career; thus they use their single status as a time of preparation for sharing their lives with a woman. They begin a savings program. They decide on the type of girl they want to marry and frequent places where they will most likely meet Miss Right.

Encouragingly, more and more churches are establishing singles groups, which sponsor programs on such themes as financial planning, parenthood and building good relationships.

3. *Creative Aloneness.* This is the route taken by men absorbed in a profession or committed to celibate religious life. It can also be an interim period for the disciplined single male who wants to avoid the pitfalls of sensual bachelorhood, is not sure he wants to be married, yet has severe doubts if lifelong chastity is possible for him. I am convinced that this is a far more viable lifestyle for the single man than our society has acknowledged.

My first awareness that there was a path of "creative aloneness" for singles came through my good friend Gene Walker. The word *celibacy* would probably have turned off both Gene and myself when we were in school together in the late '30s. An all-conference lineman on the football team, Gene was nevertheless of very different stuff from the conventional athlete. Gentle, softspoken, bluntly honest, he allied himself with unpopular causes and nettled people by opposing drinking and relaxed moral standards. In short, he was a square whom people respected but often avoided. At times I felt uncomfortable with him because he had a way of challenging me to take unpopular stands.

Although opposed to violence as an answer to anything, when our nation was attacked, Gene joined the Marines and was in the first wave of men who landed at Iwo Jima. After the war I looked him up in New York City. On a hot summer day the two of us with our dates drove over to New Jersey for a picnic. Somewhere near the picnic site, my date threw a tissue out the window of the car.

Gene, who was driving, pulled over to the side of the road, walked back a hundred yards to retrieve the white tissue, and stuffed it into a trash container in the front seat. "Please don't be offended," he said to my date with a warm smile that disarmed her. "But I've committed myself to doing everything I can to reduce litter. Just call me a fanatic."

Later, while we needled him, it was Gene who made sure that every single trace of our picnic residue was cleaned up and disposed of. After returning our dates to their women's residence hotel, Gene and I sat in a coffee shop and talked. It did not take long for us to arrive at the subject of sex and the single male. Then in his quiet, restrained manner he stretched my thinking.

"It's not necessary for bachelors to have a sex life," he said. "In fact, it hurts more than it helps."

"How does it hurt?" I asked.

"Promiscuous sex weakens us."

"But sex is a natural part of life," I protested.

"It is in its proper place—marriage. Outside of marriage it's a trap." He carefully sponged up every crumb on his plate into a last bite of cake, then gave me that thoughtful, half-humorous, half-apologetic look. "Mind you, I have the normal cravings."

"Then what's the answer for the single male with a sex drive?" I asked.

"Self-discipline."

I was disappointed. "Such as?"

A half-weary, half-dreamy expression flicked over Gene's face. "Sometimes I put on sweatpants and run until I'm exhausted. Or swim. I spend hours in the garden. I love plants. I love green growing things. I love to see beauty come out of the ground. I get on my hands and knees and weed. I dig my fingers into the soil and work until my skin's almost raw. Then I take a hot-cold shower."

I have never forgotten this image of Gene digging into the good earth until his sex fantasies ceased tormenting him. When I would describe Gene to others, there would be smirks and grimaces. "What does he do in the winter?" was one reaction. Or: "He belongs in a monastery."

While Gene did marry several years later and eventually became father to four lively youngsters, as a bachelor I think he had the key to a way of life too much scorned and overlooked in our time. Men have been assaulted, snowed and deluged under a massive media campaign—much of it dreamed up on Madison Avenue to sell everything from automobiles to shampoo—to make them feel incomplete and inadequate without a sex life. The question needs to be asked: Can a man have a good life, a creative life without sex?

The answer coming out of millions of fulfilled, productive lives through the ages is—yes.

In fact, one side effect of the recent sexplosion with its

glorification of the sex act is that more and more men are burned out and turned off, and seeking a more inclusive definition of manhood.

I recall a particular Sunday morning in December 1989, when my wife, Sandy, and I had shared the pulpit at the Tabernacle Church in Melbourne, Florida. Afterward a handsome, dark-haired young man introduced himself to me as Tony, a visitor from out of state.

"Will you pray for me?" he asked.

"Glad to. Any special need?"

He hesitated only a second. "Sexual bondage."

I found myself liking the frankness of this young man. "Is it pornography?" I guessed.

"Some. It's mostly women, though. I've been predatory."

"How old are you, Tony?"

"Twenty-two."

"How long have you been—uh, predatory?"

"Since I was fifteen. All of us were into sex early." Then his face brightened. "But I was celibate for two years."

"Tell me about that time."

"I became a Christian, went to church, made new friends, began going steady with a wonderful girl." Tears suddenly filled his eyes. "Last week we had sex for the first time. Neither one of us wanted it to happen. Now she doesn't want to see me anymore."

"Have you asked her forgiveness?"

"I've tried to, but she hangs up the phone."

As I prayed for Tony, that he would rediscover the freedom and self-worth he had found in celibacy, I was filled with an overwhelming awareness of the Lord's love for this young man—and an assurance that with God's help he and his "wonderful girl" would retrieve the relationship they'd betrayed.

Later when I shared this experience with Sandy, we marveled at how times had changed. Here was a young man of 22 already weary of the bondage that comes from the wrong use of sex. And yet it hadn't been too many years before that young people like Tony were clamoring to be free of "puritanical restraints." People wanted a sexual revolution and got it; now we are discovering that this revolution not only has not set us free, it has created a whole new set of problems.

Tony's aliveness when he mentioned his two years of celibacy has stuck with me. Have men missed something here? Does celibacy have something rich and fulfilling to offer that men need to know more about?

The Homosexual Male

What about the sizable percentage of single males who are homosexuals? Is celibacy a viable alternative for them as well?

When I began my professional career in New York City in the late 1940s, I began to be aware that certain men in my church, men whom I liked and respected as individuals were—most likely—homosexual. I never asked them if they were and they never admitted as much. For fifteen years they were simply part of a group of us that prayed together and went out socially together.

Things changed with the gay rights movement when homosexuals began to identify themselves. I was in Alaska one summer at a Christian retreat featuring superb Eskimo singing. I'll never forget the five men who rendered "How

Great Thou Art" in an Eskimo dialect as the twilight colors shifted from bright gold, to pink, to blue, to mauve. Afterward Art, a bearded man in his thirties, asked the group to pray for his special ministry to homosexuals.

It was nearly midnight when people began drifting back to their cabins. I caught up with Art on the path. "You've had experience with homosexuals," I said. "Maybe you can help me." I went on to describe a church friend whose increasingly severe problems, I felt, stemmed from his being a homosexual. "Of course I can't be sure."

"Why don't you just ask him if he's gay?"

"Just like that?" I was startled by his directness and even more so by his next statement.

"Look, I'm gay . . . have been for twenty years . . . and the only way I've gotten free from my hang-ups about my sexuality was to come into the open and say, 'O.K., world, I'm a homosexual and I'm tired of trying to hide it. Reject me if you must, but I'm going to live in freedom from now on.' "

We walked silently toward the lake as I absorbed this news. We continued our discussion sitting on one of the wooden benches of the small outdoor chapel. It was still light outside. The Alaskan summer nights were continuous twilight.

"Art, you asked us to pray for your work among gay men. Are you committed to Jesus Christ?"

"Yes, I became a Christian several years ago. We gay people need Christ just as much as you do." He paused a moment to study my face. "I now live with another man and consider myself married to him. You'd probably call him my lover, but I regard him as my spouse."

Was Art trying the shock treatment on me? I wondered.

"Since you've been so honest, I must be, too," I replied. "There are strong statements in both the Old and New Testaments against homosexuality." I quoted two of them:

> The Lord spoke to Moses, saying, . . . "You [men] shall not lie with a male as one lies with a female; it is an abomination."
>
> Leviticus 18:1, 22, NAS

> Neither fornicators, . . . nor adulterers, . . . nor homosexuals . . . shall inherit the kingdom of God.
>
> 1 Corinthians 6:9–10, NAS

"As a Christian," I asked Art, "how do you reconcile these passages with your lifestyle?"

"Paul's advice to Christians about homosexuality was for two thousand years ago," he replied. "I don't think Paul understood either sex or women. His rigidity simply isn't acceptable in the Church today. As for the passage in Leviticus, the harshness and cruelty running through the entire Old Testament makes those judgments out of date."

"By that yardstick," I said, "all standards, including the Ten Commandments and the teachings of Jesus, become relative."

Art agreed with that. "Jesus gave us guidelines. He never meant to impose a set of arbitrary laws—He fought that kind of thinking all His life. If you accept legalism, you reject the ten percent of our society who are gay."

"Art, I respect your openness and honesty. I feel I need to be that way with you. Because you are an admitted active homosexual, I feel a barrier between us and I would never want you teaching or ministering to my sons."

"That's your problem, not mine," he said, and there our conversation ended.

But not my need to wrestle with the issues he'd brought into the open. When asked some months later to team up with several other Christian writers and put together a booklet entitled "Healing for the Homosexual,"* I quickly agreed. Five of us grappled with the subject for months, researching medical opinion and studying scores of case histories, and came to the conclusion that, yes, difficult and slow as it is, healing can happen, is happening and will happen in the future to more and more homosexuals.

Christian homosexuals have two positive avenues to pursue. First, they can seek a complete inner healing and change of lifestyle from homo- to heterosexual orientation. Or, second, they can follow the path of lifelong celibacy. Any gay man who makes an all-out commitment to Jesus will be given the grace and strength and persistence to adhere successfully to one of these two routes.

A recent book, *After the Ball* by Marshall Kirk and Hunter Madsen, both gay, concludes that the homosexual revolution has failed because it focused on sexual freedom (never permissible to Christians of any stamp) instead of civil rights. They urge the 25 million American gays to "tone down and blend in," to help reestablish the community fractured when the gay rights movement became militant.

Dynamic Celibates

Jesus Christ is the greatest example of a single man who lived a dynamic celibate life. Controversy swirled about

---

* For further information, see page 251.

Jesus two thousand years ago and it still does today. Movie director Martin Scorsese is one of many "liberated moderns" offended (threatened?) by the notion that any man could live a completely pure life. His movie *The Last Temptation of Christ* portraying the Master as a weak, deluded man is a better portrait of our sexually confused and ambivalent world than of any first-century reality.

The key to a dynamic celibacy is to live a selfless life. When a man's life is centered on serving God and helping others, his energies are directed outward and there's no time to dwell on sexual hang-ups.

The apostle Paul discovered this secret. "An unmarried man can spend his time doing the Lord's work and thinking how to please him. . . . If a man has the willpower not to marry . . . he has made a wise decision. So the person who marries does well, and the person who doesn't marry does even better" (1 Corinthians 7:32, 37–38, LB).

Is Paul putting down marriage?

Not at all. He is simply holding up another commitment —an even more demanding and absorbing one: one hundred percent, all-out devotion to God. In his ministry to men, Paul is continually exhorting them to find "the best" through self-discipline, whatever their marital status: "Run from anything that gives you the evil thoughts that young men often have" (2 Timothy 2:22, LB). "For God wants you to be holy and pure, and to keep clear of all sexual sin. . . . God has not called us to be dirty-minded and full of lust, but to be holy and clean" (1 Thessalonians 4:3, 7, LB).

Celibacy in no way implies withdrawal from people or a life of seclusion. In fact, because the single person usually has fewer family responsibilities, he is freer to reach out to those around him who need his love. If I were young and single again in today's hurting world, I would opt to learn more about holy living. I would review Andrew Murray's absolute surrender, John Wesley's "second blessing" and Brother Lawrence's "practice of the presence of God" for guidelines.

The question persists: Why is the creative single life better without sex? When Gene Walker said that he was a stronger person without sexual involvements, he was speaking from personal experience. Illicit sex, excess sex can be psychologically devastating. An affair is a time-consuming, often guilt-producing, emotionally draining undertaking, not to mention the risk it brings of sexually transmitted diseases. In this area as in any other, self-indulgence results in weakness; self-denial produces strength.

A towering figure in Hebrew history, and single throughout his youth, was Joseph. Here was a man who three thousand years ago made the same discovery Gene Walker made: The more he denied himself sexual satisfaction outside of marriage, and honored the marriage bond in others, the stronger he became.

Sure, it cost him when he refused to be seduced by Potiphar's wife. This rejected woman got him thrown into jail. But there in prison began for Joseph a crucial time of self-denial and service to others that in a few years not only saw him freed from prison, but next to the king, the most powerful man in Egypt.

Roman Catholic priests are called to celibacy because the Catholic Church feels that an unmarried man can best serve his flock. Hundreds of thousands have done this selflessly and faithfully over the years. The fact that fewer men feel called to the celibate priesthood today may be because they have not been properly challenged.

I predict that as more and more men grow weary of their indulgent, self-centered, aimless lives, the emerging movement of celibate single men will grow. Jesus Christ will be its inspiration, its Guide and its power. The strength and vitality of this movement will someday astonish the world.

Questions for Reflection

1) What does celibacy mean to you personally?
2) If you were teaching about celibacy to a group of single men, what would you stress?
3) In what ways were the celibate ministries of Paul and Jesus alike—and how were they different?
4) Do you see celibacy as the best route for homosexuals who want to follow Jesus? If not, what is the answer for Christian homosexuals?
5) Most single men today believe that sexual experience before marriage is necessary. Would you challenge that belief?

3
Son

"Honor your father and mother. . . ."

Exodus 20:12, LB

Like most males during my youth and early manhood I gave little thought to what I owed my parents—or what it meant to be a son.

When I left the nest I wrote an occasional letter or card to them, called home on Mother's Day, Father's Day and other occasions. Their love for me was accepted and returned casually. Their concern and advice were often shrugged off.

The change in me began when, as the editor of *Guideposts* magazine, I took responsibility for putting together a series of articles on the Ten Commandments. Thus my first real encounter with the fifth Commandment:

> "Honor your father and mother, that you may have a long, good life in the land the Lord your God will give you."
>
> Exodus 20:12, LB

During my previous readings of this verse, I had stopped after the first five words. That seemed to say it. So I would then skip down to the sixth Commandment.

But as I lingered over the words that day in my *Guideposts* office, the totality of the promise hit me. God was giving us more than a command; He was telling us *why* it is important to honor our parents . . .

> . . . that you may have a long, good life in the land
> the Lord your God will give you.

A new thought here—that when we war with parents, reject parents or are indifferent to them we may be missing out on a special blessing.

I can hear the comments now: But you don't know what a cruel father I had. . . . My mother left my father and is a tramp. . . . My parents rejected me so why should I honor them?

The associate editor at *Guideposts* who wrote the article on the fifth Commandment was Starr West Jones. His mother, widowed when her five children were in their teens, was a most unusual woman. She loved babies, but detested sex. She was an affectionate mother, but strongly urged her children never to marry.

When eventually, one by one, her four sons did wed, she cut them off from her as though they had died. The one daughter never married and devoted her life to taking care of her mother.

Starr, a strong-minded male and an outdoor type, was the last to marry. He wanted a relationship with his mother, but was determined not to let his wife and children suffer the verbal abuse his younger brother Ted and his family had gone through when they had insisted on visiting her.

A meeting with a wise country doctor helped Starr and Ginny resolve some of their stress and pain. Impressed by the courtesy the doctor showed to his own difficult mother who lived with him and his wife, they commented on it.

"Parents," he replied, "are the instruments God used in creating us. We cannot dishonor them without dishonoring God."

Starr agreed but asked the doctor how he would handle his and Ginny's extreme situation.

"Let me ask you a question first," the doctor said. "What kind of relationship do you want with your mother?"

"A normal relationship where she accepts my wife and the children we hope to have," replied Starr. "Yet I want my actions to conform to the Commandment—without destroying the peace and integrity of our home."

"All right," said the doctor. "The fifth Commandment says honor, not obey. Now, how does the dictionary define the word *honor*?"

Starr read: "To honor is to regard with respect; to acknowledge formally as worthy of esteem and acceptance. . . ."

"Now," said the doctor, "do you expect to change your mother's views toward your marriage?"

"She'll never change in this lifetime and I will not subject my family to her verbal abuse," Starr replied.

The doctor shook his head. "Is that showing respect for her point of view?"

"It's a wrong point of view!"

"I agree," the doctor added, "but she is entitled to it. I suggest you make occasional short visits to her as a son; go by yourself. As your children grow up, take them maybe once or twice a year."

Years passed. Starr and Ginny meanwhile bought a farm in Pawling, New York, and had four sons. As suggested, Starr traveled to see his mother at her New York City apartment, brief, respectful visits.

One day while Starr and I were having lunch together I asked him how Ginny was taking this rejection.

Starr sipped his coffee for a moment. "She was hurt at first, but she accepts it now as I do, and even encourages me to visit Mother whenever I can."

Starr finished his dessert and pushed back his chair. "There was a time when I thought about removing myself totally from Mother's life. I didn't do it because I realized I would be depriving her of her right to show her love for me."

The day came when Starr visited his terminally ill mother. He and his sister sat by her bedside until she slipped away. His loving handling of this difficult relationship has borne fruit in the lives of his four sons, all of whom relate closely to their parents. Especially fascinating to me has been to watch the second part of the fifth Commandment work out in Starr's life. Now in his eighties, fully active in a writing and speaking career, still a devoted husband and father, he has reaped the promise on his farm of a long, good life.

Biblical Sons

Isaac's testing as a son on Mount Moriah is a classic example of a son's respect.

Most of the focus of this scriptural story is on Abraham, the father, and his obedience to God. Abraham heard from the Lord that he was to offer his son, Isaac, as a sacrifice. Abraham and Sarah had to wonder, "Why on earth would God ask this of us?"

Whatever questions Abraham had, he stood over his son, knife in hand, prepared to do the unthinkable.

From the son's point of view, however, the story took on a deeper dimension for me. Isaac was probably a boy in his teens. Abraham was over one hundred years old. When Isaac realized that he was to be the sacrifice on the altar at Mount Moriah, he must have been terrified. Physically, he could have torn himself away from his father; he could have pleaded and wept. Apparently he did neither. With his very life at stake, he honored his father in his role as priest.

When the Lord saw such complete trust and obedience in both father and son, He stayed Abraham's hand and a ram was substituted. *And Isaac lived a long, good life in the land the Lord gave him.*

While good things happen to the son who honors his parents, the opposite can be true of sons who are disrespectful.

An example is the biblical story about Noah and his three sons, Shem, Ham and Japheth. In his latter years the builder of the ark returned to his occupation of farming, planted a vineyard and made wine. One day Noah drank too much and passed out in his tent.

Scripture records it this way: "Ham, the father of Canaan, saw his father's nakedness and went outside and told his two brothers" (Genesis 9:22, LB). We read in Leviticus 18:7 of the Old Testament prohibition against seeing the nakedness of family members, a rule considered to be a safeguard against incest. Ham not only violated this rule but also was scornful and deriding of his father.

Shem and Japheth, on the other hand, demonstrated a respectful attitude toward their father. They backed into Noah's tent, holding a robe over their shoulders and, looking the other way, covered their father's nakedness.

When Noah awoke, he cursed Ham and his descendants and blessed Shem and Japheth, the two sons who set an example for the honoring of one's father, even when you cannot condone his behavior.

We learn from history that Ham's mockery of his father had far-reaching effects. The descendants of Ham's son Canaan, the powerful Canaanites, were later rooted out of the Promised Land by the descendants of Shem, the Israelites.

Volatile Mother, Quiet Father

As a son I was a silent critic of much that my parents did. Mother was overweight, extremely sensitive about this and other subjects, and volatile. Dad was patient, but to a fault. After upsets between them Dad would retreat to the side porch and light a cigar. I remember vividly how fiery red the front end of his cigar burned after one of their scenes.

Mealtime was the occasion of numerous upsets. The script was always the same. A remark by my father, seemingly innocuous, then a flare-up by my mother, who would explode from her chair and flounce out the front door. Dad would calmly finish his plate, excuse himself and follow her.

"What was that all about?" my sister, Pat, would ask.

I would shrug, unconcerned on the outside. Inside I was angry at Mother and her little girl tantrums, annoyed that Dad would let her do this time after time without a rebuke. He certainly wouldn't let Pat or me get away with that kind of behavior.

Soon both my parents would return to the house as though nothing had happened.

Yet I admired my mother and her talent. She was a brilliant party-giver. Also an outstanding cook. Food was an obsession with her. Sit-down dinner parties were her specialty and she controlled the dialogue about the table, bringing each person out like a maestro leading an orchestra. Mother was also an excellent writer and speaker who headed up several local and national women's groups.

My father, though an aggressive athlete in college, was gentle and quiet-spoken. He had had a stuttering problem as a boy; ever afterward the first letter of the first word he spoke in a sermon or speech or radio talk had to be *F*. Cured stutterers can wrap their lips around the letter *F* better than any other letter, he explained.

Though impressed by my father's calmness, his patience, his steadfast love for Mother, the caring heart he had for people, I regretted that he let her so dominate our home. Dad had his strengths, but I didn't see them exercised much around Mother.

In recent years as I studied the background of my heritage, my interest in my father and mother sharply increased. Why, they were fun people back in their college days!

To Howard LeSourd, my father, campus life at Ohio Wesleyan University back in 1908 was an exhilarating contrast to the restrictions of his upbringing as a son of a Methodist clergyman. As a sophomore he was attracted to a group of young campus rebels who secretly published a scandal sheet called *The Bogus*. In its pages faculty members were insulted, college traditions ridiculed, eccentric students pilloried.

Dad liked to tell this story on himself: "Five of us met secretly in one of the fraternity houses and put the copy together after midnight. We had the sheet printed at a shop far from the campus. Then late at night we sneaked into the university chapel through an unlocked window and put a copy in each hymnbook. The next day at our chapel program, *The Bogus* was a sensation."

Dad and his four confederates were caught and brought before President Herbert Welch. The president gave each a copy of *The Bogus* and asked them in turn to read the contents. How different it was hearing the crude words read aloud in this setting!

Then the president offered them the choice of dismissal from the university or a restitution program of three steps: (1) tell their parents of the episode, (2) apologize to the students at an assembly, (3) assume moral leadership on the campus from that point on.

President Welch's handling of *The Bogus* situation was a turning point for my father because having to take moral leadership on the campus led him into the ministry. Yet this turn toward more serious matters did not keep him from being attracted to the petite, irrepressible Lucile Leonard.

The daughter of a Tulsa banker, Lucile was always into mischief. While playing with matches under the front porch at age five, she set it on fire. The fire engines arrived barely in time to save the house, while Lucile watched from behind the toolshed.

Lucile hadn't been at Ohio Wesleyan very long before she and other "high spirits" living in Monnett Hall swung into action. Each day they had to walk down a hall lined with grim-faced portraits of important people: Savonarola, John Wesley and numerous bishops.

My mother and several others decided to do some face-lifting. After chewing gum furiously one evening while studying the proboscis of Cyrano de Bergerac, they crept stealthily down the hall and with surprising artistry decorated the nose on each portrait with wads of gum. The result was so hilarious that the stern-faced dean of women summoned school officials to view the portraits before she carefully removed the gum.

Lucile was a freshman when she met Howard, already graduated, at a basketball game. Although Lucile was bored by sporting events, from then on she seldom missed attending one. When Howard decided to take theological training at a liberal seminary, Lucile had to face the fact that she was going to be what she had vowed as a teenager never to be—the wife of a preacher.

Two individuals, two different backgrounds. It was to be many years, and a lot of living, before I was able to appreciate the strength of the bond between them.

Father Figures

When a son outgrows childhood, he does not outgrow his need for a father. If he lives a distance from his own parents, another older man can fill that role. Throughout my young adult years I was blessed with a series of outstanding father figures.

Branch Rickey, the man who did so much to develop major league baseball and who coached my father at Ohio Wesleyan back in 1911, appeared in my life at various times. During World War II when I was taking a radio operator's course at Scott Field near St. Louis and was struggling with various temptations, Mr. Rickey would invite me to spend weekends with his family. Then he would pepper me with questions about my goals and standards, making me most uncomfortable in the process, but leaving a residue of unforgettable memories.

Fulton Oursler, a senior editor at the *Reader's Digest* in the '40s and early '50s, was a father figure to me as a writer-editor. His wife, Grace Perkins Oursler, was executive editor of *Guideposts* for several years at a time when I was associate editor. Fulton was ruthless with my work.

Once he asked to see an article I was writing. It was late afternoon when I finished it, and the result was too hastily done and inadequately thought through. The next morning he asked me to come to his office.

"Len, about that article you sent me last night. Don't ever again make me read something so poorly prepared."

Ouch! I groped for an excuse, could find none, so meekly admitted he was right. Then Fulton took the time to show me how it should have been prepared. He did it dramatically, walking back and forth behind his desk, crackling out sentences that I struggled frantically to get down on paper.

"Begin the article this way," he said. "It was midnight— and the phone was ringing. . . ." He paused, intense eyes piercing me. "This way the reader's immediately into the story, eager to know what's going to happen."

Fulton was not my employer, nor was he acting as my friend. He cared more for me than that —he was the stern father at that point in my life when my real father was many miles away.

A third father figure was Norman Vincent Peale, who hired me as a reporter at *Guideposts*, understood and shared my aversion to religiosity, overlooked my independent behavior and had infinite patience with my editing of his copy. He also steered me to the young adult group of his Marble Collegiate Church in New York City where I met my fourth father figure, Harold Brinig.

Harold, fifty, was a printing salesman but he along with his wife, Mary, majored in helping confused young people. The moment he saw me walking into the basement of the church, he knew he had a new prospect. I was 28, single and definitely confused.

A Weekend at Ramapo

Each Thursday night there was a program, refreshments and dancing. The strategy was to attract young people through entertainment, then get them involved in the spiritual life of the church. The second time I showed up Harold asked me some questions, then posed this one: "Would you like to join a group of us on a weekend retreat next month?"

I was wary. "What do you mean 'retreat'? I don't like to retreat from anything."

A look of amusement crossed his face. "Let's not call it a retreat, then, but an 'advance.' The purpose of this weekend is to have some fellowship together away from the city."

"Let me think about it," I said. I liked these young people. They were not as hip as the friends I had there in New York before the war, but that whole crowd was gone, scattered throughout the country, I guessed.

On a Friday afternoon in late May, 26 of us crowded into cars for the two-hour drive from mid-Manhattan across the Hudson River to Ramapo, New York, not far from the New Jersey line. Among us were young executives of both sexes, secretaries, typists, an auto mechanic, a tugboat operator, a Wall Street broker, a dress designer, an accountant, an editor, plus assorted students.

That night we gathered in a spacious lounge at the retreat center for our first meeting. Right away I knew I was in trouble. The focus of the weekend was on "Commitment to Jesus Christ." I had joined the church at age ten but this was not what they were talking about. I quickly calculated what would happen if I slipped out of the meeting, grabbed my suitcase and drove back to New York alone. Then I sighed. If I did that, the people who came with me might not have rides back to the city. Grimly, I hunkered down for a miserable weekend.

By dinnertime Saturday night, however, I had relaxed a bit. Fun and recreation were mixed in with the meetings. To my surprise, Harold Brinig played a strong third base in a softball game. At age fifty!

As we left the field, Harold put a sweaty hand on my shoulder and with that disarming smile said, "Len, we all love you."

A knot of hardness was beginning to dissolve inside me.

By the time the Saturday evening meeting started, two opposing forces inside me were in mortal combat.

One side said, *You don't belong here, Len. You don't share the beliefs of these fanatics.*

The other said, *Your life's a mess, Len. When are you going to do something about it?*

During the meeting one person after another described how a life run by the Lord freed them from past bondages. Harold's wife, Mary, summed it up by reading this statement of Jesus to His disciples: "Ye have not chosen me, but I have chosen you . . . that ye should go and bring forth fruit" (John 15:16 KJV).

"How exciting to think that Christ is choosing each one of us to be a disciple for Him in New York City," she concluded.

The meeting ended and I escaped out into the night, walking aimlessly, my emotions churning. Then I discovered myself at a nearby chapel.

It was a simple, crudely furnished room with folding chairs for about twenty. Up front was an altar, behind that a picture of Christ with outstretched arms. Memories flooded me of times I had fled emotional situations . . . ever since that afternoon at the movies when I was twelve. *Cool it, Len,* one of the voices said. *Get out of this place and tomorrow you'll be yourself again.*

The other voice argued, *Jesus wept. And He is the strongest of all.*

Then the first voice took another tack. *Don't kneel! That's surrender of your manhood.*

For a long moment I stood there, frozen in time, aware of the shallowness of my self-centered life, hating it, wanting forgiveness for it, seeing a vision of something so much more worthwhile—if I took this next step.

My knees bent. As I knelt and looked up into the face of Jesus, the dam inside me broke. Tears flowed for the first time in seventeen years. In a stumbling prayer I asked Him to take over my life.

When we all met the next morning for breakfast, Harold came up and put his arm around me. "Do you have something to report to the group, Len?"

"How did you know?"

"It's on your face."

When I told these new friends about my experience the night before, the tears came again—this time washing away some self-imposed barrier, making genuine friendship possible for the very first time.

Several years later I was asked to give testimony to my changed life at a Sunday night meeting of this same young adult group. By this time my father had retired as dean of the School of Communications at Boston University. He and Mother had moved to New York City where Dad began to work part-time for several Christian organizations.

The night of the testimony I was just getting up to speak when I saw my parents taking seats at the rear of the auditorium. Rattled, I wondered whether I should change my speech. Would it seem to them a reproach to my upbringing in a Christian home to state publicly that Jesus had never been real to me before that night at Ramapo? An inner nudging seemed to prompt me to speak as I had planned.

After I finished Dad and Mother slipped away before I had a chance to greet them. Several days later I stopped at their apartment. I could tell that Mother was upset with me.

Dad's attitude, however, was warm and loving. "You gave a powerful witness, son, and I'm proud of you."

Role Reversal

With my parents semi-retired, a new relationship between us evolved. They became more and more dependent on me. My financial situation had improved; theirs had declined. For the first time I was able to help them in this way.

But it went deeper than that. They sought my advice. One summer Mother suffered a heart attack at their summer place in Maine and was rushed to the General Hospital in Portland. Upon arriving at her bedside, I was distressed by my father's confusion and fatigue. She desperately needed his strength, but at age eighty, he seemed to have little to give except an almost mute willingness to try and do everything she asked. I ached for them both. Mother's first request when she came out of the ether after a pacemaker had been inserted inside her chest was, "I want a Bible." I learned that she had gone into the operation with a quarter in her fist so that the words *In God We Trust* were pressed against her flesh.

When the nurse came to bathe Mother, I suggested to my father that we go somewhere and talk. We found a small, unoccupied waiting room.

Our roles were reversed. The son was now the father. I sat facing him, wondering how to handle this new situation.

"Mother really surprises me," I began.

"How do you mean?"

"The quarter in her fist. Quite creative. And her eagerness to have a Bible."

"We've read the Bible together more than you realize."

"Tell me about it."

Somewhat reluctantly, he described the morning times when they'd prayed together and read Scripture. Again I wondered how my father could set such a wonderful example of loving concern for others, could show such infinite patience with people's mistakes, and yet have difficulty sharing his own deep personal beliefs.

Then I asked a question that had been on my mind for some time. "Does Mother believe in an afterlife?"

"Yes."

Dad was silent for a long moment. "She has always been fearful of death, though."

"Why?"

"I think she just hates the idea of leaving this world."

"Doesn't she believe we'll all meet in the next world?"

"Yes."

There was a gulf between us and I felt my words had been inadequate, even judgmental.

"Dad, I'm trying to be helpful because I love you and Mother very much. Mother seems to need reassurance at a deep level and I think only you can give it to her."

"In what way?"

"In terms of your faith."

There was another uncomfortable silence. "Len, I've failed her in many ways over the years. What should I say to her?"

I took a deep breath. "When I was a boy, I used to be afraid of death. I was afraid it was eternal nothingness.

69

The possibility that I could become forever extinct frightened me terribly.

"When I asked you about this, I remember your answer very clearly. You told me that if God could create the amazing and tremendously complex human being, then He certainly had the power to take care of His creations after death. That helped me a lot."

A tear trickled slowly down my father's cheek. My eyes suddenly blurred. Dad had indeed ministered faith to me as a boy. I reached over and put my hand on his. We sat silently. The gulf between us was gone.

Mother rallied from her heart attack, helped a great deal by my father's daily ministry to her needs. I returned to my life's routines. Then on September 8, 1972, came a telephone call to Florida from my sister, who was visiting our parents.

"Dad died an hour ago," she said. "He turned over in bed early this morning, put his arm around Mother, sighed and was gone." He was 84. A flood of emotions surged through me.

I was touched by the hundreds of people who came to my father's funeral service held at the Marble Collegiate Church. He was loved by so many. Mother fell apart, hardly able to function.

I arranged for burial at the family plot in the Hillside Cemetery outside of Bethany, Ohio. Since Mother was not well enough to go to the graveside service, I asked my son Chet, then a college sophomore, to meet me at the Indianapolis Airport.

It was so right. My father had often played catch with Chet when he was a boy, taught him to fish in the cold ocean off the coast of Maine. Now for a special moment three generations of LeSourd men were together, two in the flesh, one in the spirit. Chet and I, plus a half-dozen Ohio relatives, listened to the words of the minister, watched the coffin lowered into the ground under the hot September sun.

It was an important time for my nineteen-year-old son. His deep brown eyes were reflective. "Grandfather was so unselfish."

I nodded and then I saw it. The strengths I had looked for in my father were there all the time. He was always the strong one, even in what I saw as weakness.

Mother lived another thirteen years at a retirement center in Gaithersburg, Maryland. The last few years she was comatose. I would sit by her bed, staring at her silent form, wondering what I could do except pray for her.

During one visit I decided just to talk to her as though she could hear me. "Mother, do you remember the train parties you used to have in our Newton home? The whole house was divided up into separate cars. People got tickets punched when they arrived, had a choice of sitting in the parlor car or observation car or dining car or caboose. Entertainment took place in the aisles; guests would write telegrams to those in other cars, delivered by the chief porter, Dad. I couldn't believe all the laughter and fun you had. All without any alcohol, too."

I was chatting away in this vein when suddenly I stopped talking and stared at her face. She still had not moved. Her eyes were still closed. But tears were sliding down each cheek. She had heard me!

When Mother died at 93, my daughter, Linda, joined me for a small service. All Mother's friends and contemporaries were gone, except just a handful at the retirement center. As we listened to the pastor read Scripture, I kept hearing the words *Honor your father and mother.* . . . *Honor your father and mother.*

How rich the benefits when one obeys that Commandment!

Questions for Reflection

1) How does the fifth Commandment relate to your life today?
2) What is the best way to handle a role reversal between father and son? Mother and daughter?
3) What responsiblity does a son have when there is a marital rift or divorce between his parents?
4) How do you pray for the father figure you need at various junctures in your life?
5) The eighteenth chapter of Leviticus, with its emphasis on covering the nakedness of family members, has been scorned by many as completely out of date. Does all the incest coming to light today justify these prohibitions?

4
Lover

How beautiful you are, my love . . . ! Your eyes are
those of doves. . . . Your lips are like a thread of scar-
let. . . .

Song of Solomon 4-1, 3, LB

Men yearn to be good lovers. But do they know that
their rush to have sex can be the enemy of romance? And
of their creativity as lovers?

A few years ago I was wondering what had happened to
creativity in romance, when it exploded all about me.

In 1984 my younger son, Jeffrey, was living in St. Louis,
working for the telephone company and preparing himself for marriage—even though he had not yet met the
right girl. When he was about to buy a four-bedroom
house, I tried to convince him that this was a mistake, that
as a bachelor he needed only a small place; he should be
flexible in his living situation. Jeff disagreed.

"Owning a house will force me to learn how to take care
of it. Furthermore, if I own a house instead of renting, I'm
building up equity."

He was right in this situation. I was wrong.

Meanwhile Jeff was searching for the right mate. During

his twenties there were a number of candidates; none worked out. When he reached thirty I began to be a bit concerned for him. He was good husband and father material. Was he being too choosy?

At this stage in my life I had been a widower for over a year, desperately missing the close creative relationship Catherine and I had experienced for 23 years. My prayer went something like this: "Lord, You were such a great matchmaker back in 1959 when you brought Catherine and me together. Would you do it again for me in 1984? And for Jeff?"

Soon afterward I met Sandra Simpson at a writers' workshop. Though she had gone through some painful years before becoming a believer, she captivated me with her enthusiasm for life. Later while I was on a trip to New England, she and I had our first date—a dinner together at the Trapp Family Lodge in Stowe, Vermont. During dinner she invited me to have dessert at her house in nearby Montpelier. By now I was feeling a strong physical attraction to this very vibrant and warm-hearted woman.

When we entered her home at about ten o'clock I wondered what kind of signal I was receiving from Sandy. I soon found out. As she showed me about her house, we stopped at a hearth in her living room.

"This is where I serve myself Communion," she said.

"You take Communion by yourself?"

"Yes, I find it a beautiful time of intimacy with the Lord." She studied me for a moment. "Would you like to have Communion here with me now?"

I was startled, but only for a moment. Something was beginning to work inside me. Sandy brought the elements from the kitchen— a goblet of grape juice, two small wafers. We knelt together, served each other "the bread of life," then "the cup of salvation."

I took her hand and heard myself praying, "Lord, we are Your children, committed to You, eager to have You in charge of this relationship."

He heard our prayer. We were given clear instructions how to conduct our courtship so that two people falling in love could really get to know each other. We were to take time to meet with every member of both families and win them. We were to be guided by Scripture. This way He would be in charge and ours would be a most creative romance.

And it was. So much more so than if we had been in charge. When the Lord is in it, unexpected and delightful surprises are always happening.

Jeff, meanwhile, was a keen observer of Sandy and my ten-month courtship, with the marriage taking place June 22, 1985. He agreed that he was ready to let God be the matchmaker in his life, too. We all soon learned how differently God works in each situation.

Jeff met Nancy Oliver by telephone. Nancy was a lawyer in Washington. Jeff had been referred to her on a business matter. They enjoyed talking with each other on the phone so much that their long-distance conversation went on every night for the next fourteen days—a total of fifty hours. Was it building to a romance?

When Jeff flew to Washington two weeks later and met Nancy face-to-face a strong physical attraction was missing. Too bad!

But wait! When Jeff returned to St. Louis he called Nancy again. The phone conversation continued on and on. A joint conclusion: They truly enjoyed talking to each other. Why wasn't there a physical spark?

When Jeff and Nancy both took time to reexamine their past experience and approaches to romance, they made significant discoveries. Their spirits had fallen in love. But physically Nancy had always been attracted to tall, handsome, sophisticated Ivy League men, who ended up disillusioning her. Jeff was not tall; he had attended a small Midwestern college; he rejected the pseudo-sophisticated manner for a much more straightforward approach.

As for Jeff, he had visions of a soft, submissive type. Nancy was attractive, but confrontational, intellectual.

They met again, battled, talked nonstop. At one point when both were frustrated, Jeff stated, "I'm not exactly your knight in shining armor, am I."

Nancy conceded that was true.

Jeff sighed. "Well, you're no submissive fair maiden, either."

They laughed and kept digging in on who they really were. They spent one whole day together reading and discussing a book on the subject of why women so often fall for the wrong men.

When they began praying together, they fell in love.

Then came that memorable Saturday afternoon in April 1986. Jeff had been given an idea that got him on the phone with every costume house in Washington, D.C., before he found what he wanted. He invited Nancy for dinner, asked her to wear "a formal dress you would have worn at a medieval ball."

"Is this a costume party?" Nancy asked.

"Sort of," was all Jeff would say.

They met at Evergreen Farm, home to Sandy and me in

northern Virginia and the gathering place for family events. Nancy arrived late Saturday afternoon in an old-fashioned green formal dress. Jeff asked Sandy to take Nancy outside to the front lawn and sit on the wrought-iron love seat, while he and I dealt with his costume.

A half hour later the front door of the farmhouse opened and a figure emerged, walked across the porch and down the lawn toward the two women.

When Nancy looked up, she saw striding toward her a medieval knight, wearing visored black helmet with purple plume, silver coat of armor that came to his knees, high black boots. In one hand he carried a golden lance; in the other a box wrapped in green paper.

Sandy disappeared behind a bush to take pictures while Nancy stared in disbelief. The knight stopped in front of Nancy, then knelt.

"Your knight in shining armor has arrived to seek your hand in marriage."

Then he unwrapped the box. In it was a lady's white glove. On the ring finger was the blue sapphire engagement ring I had given Catherine at this very same farm 32 years before. After Catherine's death it had been given to Jeff.

As Nancy said yes to the proposal, tears in her eyes, Jeff took the ring off the glove and slipped it onto her finger.

That night people in a nearby restaurant were astonished to see a couple arrive for dinner, the man in full knight's armor, the bride-to-be showing off her sparkling engagement ring.

Jeff and Nancy's wedding took place October 18, 1986, at the Church of the Nazarene in Leesburg, Virginia. Just before the wedding was to start, the two hundred assembled guests were startled to see the groom stride to the front of the church to make an announcement.

"There is a behind-the-scenes story about this wedding that you should know," Jeff began. "One of my greatest dreams as a boy was that my stepmother, Catherine Marshall, who raised me from the age of three, would know and love my bride. When Mom died four-and-a-half years ago, I grieved that this could never happen.

"Well, I was wrong. Mom had already met Nancy. It happened back in 1974 at Agnes Scott College when Nancy was a student there. She was given the assignment to escort Catherine, who was then an Agnes Scott board member, about the grounds on alumni day. So my bride did meet my stepmother. And you know what—God has been so much a part of this courtship that I'm sure He has arranged for Mom to be here in spirit today."

Such creativity in a lover could originate only from the Lord of creativity Himself!

How Sweet Your Love!

I have always been both delighted and astonished at these romantic words leaping forth from the Holy Book:

> "How beautiful you are, my love, how beautiful!
> Your eyes are those of doves. . . .
> Your teeth are white as sheep's wool, newly shorn
>   and washed; . . .
> Your lips are like a thread of scarlet—and how
>   beautiful your mouth.
> Your cheeks are matched loveliness. . . .
> You are so beautiful, my love, in every part of you."

At first glance this reads like prose from a modern love story. In fact, it was written thousands of years ago by a lover to his bride. That words so passionate and descriptive could come from the Bible confounds many people.

Why should we be surprised? As the creator of romance, why wouldn't God want such beautiful, endearing expressions of love in His Word?

> "You have ravished my heart, my lovely one,
>   my bride;
> I am overcome by one glance of your eyes,
>   by a single bead of your necklace.
> How sweet is your love, my darling. . . .
> How much better it is than mere wine.
> The perfume of your love is more fragrant
>   than all the richest spices.
> Your lips, my dear, are made of honey. . . .
> My darling bride is like a private garden,
>   a spring that no one else can have,
>   a fountain of my own."
>   Song of Solomon 4:1–12, LB

I wonder how many men would think of reading these words to their brides on their wedding night? I have not seen statistics on how brides rate husbands' "romance factor" in today's world, but my guess is it would not be very high.

During an honest sharing session with a group of couples at a recent Marriage Encounter weekend, most admitted that the first night of their marriage was not only disappointing, but in some cases a total disaster.

One bride threw up all night long.

One new husband passed out in the car and had to be carried to the honeymoon suite.

Another bride was so angry with her husband's insensitivity she left their room and sat in the hotel lobby the rest of the night.

Several couples were so exhausted they fell asleep either in the middle of the sex act or before it could happen. (It was generally agreed that there should be no effort to consummate the marriage that first night; that the couple should get a good night's sleep and take up romance the next day.)

Those couples who had been living together or were having regular sex before marriage did not have much to say. Privately, several of the women conceded that their wedding night was the occasion for some angry words, prompted usually by the husband's taking this romantic event so casually.

Men—let's face it. If romance is in a state of decline today, it's mostly our fault.

Go to a secular bookstore, notice how many sections are given over to romance books, and you will understand why sales of romance fiction today are at an all-time high. In research Sandy and I have done on compulsive behavior, we discovered there is a new kind of addiction on the part of women, and women alone—paperback romance novels. Women buy them in bunches and hide them about the house from their husbands. They become closet readers, sometimes rising during the night or early morning to get their romance fix. Husbands seldom know what is happening. Alcohol, drugs, food, shopping binges they might understand, but romance novels!

Most males do not want to understand. If they did, they

would feel indicted for affection deprivation. Television shows today produce almost a caricature of the unromantic male who awakens each morning with his work agenda on his mind. Children may get a hug, more often words of admonishment or rebuke. The wife will receive a pat on the bottom or a hurried good-bye kiss.

After work the man returns tired, cross. He reads the paper and his mail, watches the news and seldom is communicative at dinner. Evenings, after the children are asleep, he sits in front of the television until time to go to bed.

Any variety to this routine is usually sparked by the woman. She will set up a dinner party, a visit with friends or plans for a church program. If the man doesn't like the plan, he will beg off with the excuse he has to work, whether he really needs to or not. I know. I have often used work as an excuse to duck shopping or a town meeting or something else I didn't want to do.

No wonder so many women attached to unromantic men become addicts to alcohol, drugs, eating, shopping or romance novels.

A woman who heard me describe men today as unromantic said, "You're wrong—my husband and I have been married thirty-eight years and he still romances me the way he did when we were first married."

Another woman described a good-bye scene with her husband at the airport. He went through the metal detector, walked a good fifty yards to his gate, then turned around to wave again and shouted, "I love you."

As his voice exploded through the airport, everyone turned to look. And smile. Here was a man who truly loved his wife—and didn't care who knew it.

There are many good male lovers today, of course. Old-fashioned romance is not dead, just in a state of decline.

On the other extreme is a breed of men who are such skillful lovers (or seducers) that they end up as sexaholics. Peter Trachtenberg, a bachelor in his late thirties, describes himself as "a recovering Casanova" and has written a book about this sickness called *The Casanova Complex.*

Some men have continual sexual experiences as they search for just the right partner. The Casanova type never stops searching, Trachtenberg warns. "Any woman who loves him will be just one in a series of women, and she can't cure him by loving him." He divides the compulsive lovers into six types:

> *Hitters.* They are the Don Juans on a ruthless search for sexual partners who plan their exits before they enter a bedroom and never fall in love.
>
> *Drifters.* These James Bonds remain in command of their feelings and responses. Even in the bedroom they are stirred but not shaken. Women come on to them and the chase is their turn-on. They leave when they get bored.
>
> *Romantics.* The most appealing of the Casanovas. They resemble the dramatic, tormented dream man of the Gothic novel. They charm women and fall in love—and out—because they envision love without conflict.
>
> *Nesters.* The Ernest Hemingway type. They seek deep and lasting relationships but are ter-

rified by intimacy and soon withdraw. They have several ex-wives.

Jugglers. They always have two women in their lives. Obsessed with control, they have a mortal terror of attachment and walk away from their women without regret.

Tomcats. These are the most common Casanovas. They marry and may stay with a partner for life, but they are never faithful and have many other partners. Their womanizing frequently surfaces at times when they feel especially close to their wives.

To become free from his sexual bondage, Trachtenberg has spent five years in psychotherapy and Twelve-Step programs for sexual addiction and co-dependency.

The warning to men (and women) is to avoid creating an aura about yourself that somehow you are a victim of "many heartless shrews" and therefore need a woman who understands you. This is a sexual trap for yourself and any woman you meet.

My conclusion after studying this report: A truly great lover is the man who can satisfy one woman all her life and be satisfied by her.

Why Men Are Less Romantic

There are three reasons (probably more) why men are less romantic today.

First, television. Watching the tube night after night drains a man's vitality, stifles his desire, turns him into a couch potato.

Second, the sexplosion. As a result of the loosening of sexual barriers, men get obsessed with self-gratification and become determined to "get theirs" like everyone else. As a result men become takers instead of givers.

Third, pornography. It will be years before we can calculate the damage done by the massive onslaught of hard porn and X-rated films on both men and women. There is solid evidence that pornography has caused men to commit serious crimes against women. Harder to prove is that pornography destroys marriages by causing one or both partners to become dissatisfied with their marital sex and thus turn to the fantasy life they can get in pornography.

The explosion of pornography in magazines and on films began in the early 1970s. On the way to my New York City office I could hardly avoid the salacious titles on newsstands: "Check Out Your Sexual Prowess" . . . "The Kind of Lover Every Woman Wants" . . . "Wife-Swapping Can Revive Your Marriage."

One morning while at an editorial conference in another city during the mid-1970s, I awoke nursing a good case of self-pity. There had been an upsetting call the night before with Catherine. I felt her criticism of me was unfair.

Looking through the newspaper that morning, I met a barrage of advertisements for X-rated films. With my barriers down, the erotic copy reached me at an emotional level, resurrecting images I thought I had dealt with years before. My mind compromised in this way:

"I really ought to see one of these films," I rationalized. "If this is Satan at work, then as an editor of a religious magazine, I should be able to understand his methods."

I selected the film that had received the most publicity. The minute I walked up to the ticket counter that afternoon, a feeling of furtiveness took hold of me. I avoided looking into anyone's face. I took a rear seat in the theatre. When my conscience stirred, I steeled myself: *You are here on a professional mission.*

That professionalism disappeared when the film began. I found it easy to be fairly objective about nudity. Naked bodies are just not that mysterious. But the male sexual encounters with the female were something else. At one point something inside said, *Get up and leave.*

I ignored this, preferring to wallow in the onslaught of images on my mind. There was no beauty, no depth of characterization, no redeeming intrinsic values. It was a film made with the express purpose of stirring up one's lust. It did mine.

When the film was over and I walked out of the theatre, I felt unclean. The feeling of being soiled persisted when I returned to my hotel room. Scenes of passion and eroticism kept reappearing in my mind like a series of camera impressions—a montage of sensual mouths, leering eyes, body parts moving in response to primitive emotions. I let the shower soak my head for a long time. Water did not erase the images in my brain.

My rational mind assured me that the assault was only temporary, that the experience would fade quickly, that I had enough strength of will to push it aside. I am sure this was true, but I wanted a cleansing, not a gradual fading of the memory. More than that, I began to feel a smoldering anger building up inside. Why do we humans despoil beauty? Why do we take a lovely God-created act between husband and wife and make it ugly?

On my knees by the bed I laid it all on the altar: my phony rationalization, my hypocrisy, my lust, my self-pity. "How do You stand us, Lord?" I asked. "Forgive me for leaving You and consorting with the enemy."

Now I am sure there are people, even Christians, who will say, "Come on, Len. You're making too big a deal out of this. X-rated films aren't that harmful."

They miss the point. If there is a way to measure sins from "mortal" to "venal," this one may not be at the top. Yet through a deliberate act I opened myself to the spirit of lust. The result was harmful to me and my marriage until I went through a cleansing process. And the truth is—lust always destroys the fragile quality of romance.

What Women Prefer

Several years ago Ann Landers asked her millions of female readers which they preferred from their men: cuddling or sex. The response, she said, was "a stunner." Of more than 90,000 who responded, some 64,000 said, "A warm hug or gentle loving touch is more important than intercourse."

"This survey," reported Landers, "tells me that there is a lot of dissatisfaction among women. They're full of rage, anger, guilt and don't hesitate to write about it. When so many women respond so earnestly, so passionately, so honestly, it means I've hit a real hot button."

Typical response:

"I'm under forty and would be delighted to settle for tender words and warm caresses. The rest of it is a bore and can be exhausting. I'm sure the sex act was designed strictly for the pleasure of males."

Could it be that we males grew up with all the wrong ideas of what most women are looking for in romance?

Somewhere along the way I decided that you never gave your hand away with a woman, that she wanted a man to be mysterious, an enigma, difficult to pin down. Perhaps all this came from an unreal world of motion pictures in the '30s, '40s, '50s. The end result was my learning the art of gamesmanship and deception in romancing a woman.

The problem was—this is not the best way to find your right mate.

After an unsuccessful first marriage, I sought help from the Lord. The Author of creativity in romance gave me a two-word answer—*Try honesty.*

Honesty in romance? How could that possibly work? I wasn't sure I could change, but I vowed to try.

When in 1959 I began courting Catherine Marshall, a woman whose religious books had inspired millions, we seemed such an unlikely match. Her first marriage to Peter Marshall seemed heaven-inspired and was ended by his sudden death. I found it terribly daunting even to try to follow that great act.

Yet something special happened to us that warm August day Catherine and I spent together, mostly talking, as we drove and picnicked off Skyline Drive in Northern Virginia. Though we found a few other occasions to be together for short periods after that, and talked daily on the telephone, we were not at all sure where it was going when Catherine came to my home in Carmel, New York, to be with me and my children for a weekend.

It was late on a Friday evening when Catherine and I said good-bye to several neighbors and walked out alone into a moonlit yard, holding hands. I was by now in love with Catherine and uncertain how to proceed.

I put my arm around her, drew her to me and kissed

her. A first kiss. An electric moment. How good it felt to hold her in my arms.

I pulled up two wicker chairs and we sat down, still holding hands. Now it was time for some light romantic. talk, I figured. The old Len was ready to start playing games. But the new Len broke through. Words flowed out that were not at all what I intended.

"Catherine, do you believe that in some supernatural way two people can be brought together almost against their wills?"

"If you're asking me does God violate our human will, then I would have to say I don't think so." Catherine was silent a moment. "Why do you ask?"

"I've been trying to learn something about the way we get guidance from God," I answered hesitantly. "I know He gives us free will to accept or reject Him. Yet God really zapped Paul on the Damascus road when Paul was not seeking Him at all."

"But Paul was probably tormented on the inside. We don't know that he wasn't miserable in his persecution of Christians and thus crying for help."

"Yet Paul seemed so convinced that he was doing the right thing when *wham, bang, crash!* He was knocked flat on the ground by the power of the Lord. This example of supernatural intervention into man's affairs has always seemed a kind of overkill."

"I agree it isn't the way God usually deals with us. There are times He intervenes directly in our lives." Catherine looked at me reflectively. "Has this happened to you?"

I squirmed uncomfortably in my chair, kicking myself mentally for shifting the mood in such a ponderously philosophical way, wishing I was still kissing her instead of talking. "No and yes," I answered, struggling. "No, in that the Lord hasn't blinded me with a great light. Yes, in that I feel He has brought you and me together in a supernatural way."

"How?"

"One night months ago I was in a terrible state. Everything was going wrong. I was trying to enjoy myself at parties, but was feeling miserable and guilty about leaving the children. And I was far away from God. So this night I sort of crept back to Him, asked His forgiveness and help. And asked for a new marriage partner. It was after this prayer that your name flashed into my mind."

Silence. Catherine was looking at me intently. I felt completely unsure of myself. Why was I saying these things?

"I know I'm mixed up," I heard myself continuing. "Part of me wants to be free of problems and burdens. Yes, to be free of religious restraints, too. Sometimes I'm full of self-pity having three young children to raise by myself and all the housekeeper trouble. Then another part of me wants to take on even more responsibility, yearns to know God in a more intimate way. That's the part of me strongly drawn to you, Catherine. That part of me wants to tell you how much I need you in my life."

I stopped talking for a moment and considered with dismay what I had just said. Why was I going out on a limb this way? *You fool,* I thought. *You're moving too fast. Cool it. Lighten things up. Try some banter. Go anywhere but this direction.*

Yet to my surprise, I heard myself continuing in the

same vein. "I know I'm being too outspoken, but playing games with you is suddenly distasteful to me. I've done that most of my life in my relationships with women and it hasn't worked out right. It's been phony. I'm tired of phoniness. I want honesty. I also very much want you. You probably think I'm naïve or silly or immature to talk like this so soon after we've begun seeing each other. Perhaps so. I surprise myself."

"No, Len, I don't think you're silly or immature. Impulsive, perhaps. We really don't know a lot about each other."

"Perhaps not. Yet deep down I feel I know you in a way I've never known anyone else. I can see the Lord really using us as a team. It scares me, but it excites me. I didn't know how sure I was until I opened my mouth."

"Len, have you any idea how far out on a limb you've gone?"

There was a long silence while the two forces within me struggled. *You've blown the whole evening, you dope.*

"Catherine, it's late and I got carried away. I'm sorry."

Now Catherine became intense. "Look here, Len. You startled me. You've even shocked me. But by deliberately making yourself so open and vulnerable, you have touched me—more than you realize."

Amazing how God works! He led me to Catherine, and then in spite of my inner resistance, He gave me the words that somehow disarmed her, touched her heart. In the process He showed me how effective a male lover can be when he becomes honest instead of devious.

From then on I sensed the Lord was in charge of our romance. We were married four months later.

*   *   *

How good a lover are you?

Remember that those who esteem themselves as good lovers are often too egotistical to be able to give themselves totally in a love relationship. They tend to think of immediate results of self-gratification, not of building a relationship that lasts.

Good lovers learn to get self out of the way. That's why a "let go and let God" approach works so much better. When "self" is in control there is desire and intensity; when the Lord is King He brings surprises, inner delight, joy, humor, a kind of relaxed power to romance.

Try something new today. Tell your sweetheart you have a special message for her. Find the right time and place. Relax. Then make the Song of Solomon a special love letter to her:

"How beautiful you are, my love . . .
Your eyes are those of doves . . .
You have ravished my heart."

Questions for Discussion

1) Can you give a good example in real life or fiction of a romantic man? What makes him special this way?
2) When God is in charge of a romantic courtship, what is different about it?
3) What scriptural guidelines are there for a romance relationship? Can you name specific verses?
4) Do you recognize the "Casanova Complex"

in yourself? How do you cope with it in yourself? In someone else?

5) If a man about to be married approached you
for advice on how to plan his honeymoon
night, what would you suggest?

5
Husband

Husbands, love your wives, just as Christ also loved
the church and gave Himself up for her.

Ephesians 5:25, NAS

A few weeks before the wedding of my son, Jeff, and
Nancy back in 1987, he asked me if I would be willing
early in the ceremony to make a brief statement to the
assembled guests.

"A statement?" I questioned.

"Yes. That I'm ready to become a good husband," Jeff
grinned.

"How long a statement?"

"Five minutes or so."

Emotions began bubbling inside me as I agreed. After
three marriages what had I learned about being a husband
that I could share with his wedding guests? In five minutes? Not an easy assignment.

The crux of my message to the bride and groom was
this:

"Nancy and Jeff, you need to see your marriage as a
triangle. God is at the apex. He is in charge. As husband

and wife you two are at the lower corners. Both of you are equal in His sight; you are both committed to Him and to each other. Thinking of your marriage as a triangle will keep your relationship in balance.

"As the husband, Jeff, you are the spiritual head of your home. This is the mantle God places upon your head. You are to love your wife just as Christ loved the Church and gave Himself up for her."

I spoke for several minutes, but little I could say—particularly to Jeff—would be more important than that verse from Ephesians. A husband needs to measure the love he has for his wife by the love Christ has for the Church, remembering that *He gave Himself up for her.* That is sacrificial love. I can see so clearly now that it was missing in my first marriage. . . .

On a raw February night back in 1948 I debated whether to go to a movie or to the young adult program at the Marble Collegiate Church in New York City where some kind of variety show was scheduled. I was not much into churchgoing, but I went to the variety show.

The mistress of ceremonies was a stunning brunette named Eve. She was personable and witty. She was a model, I discovered, and her picture had been on the cover of one of the glamour magazines. I decided I wanted to get to know Eve.

In the months that followed Eve and I dated regularly. Though attracted to each other, we were both struggling to find ourselves. It was during that May that I went on the weekend retreat at Ramapo and had my life turned around. Eve had already been through the same kind of experience. We seemed more right for each other now and became engaged.

Yet there was a lot we both had not dealt with. I was on the right track spiritually, but my lifestyle had not changed much. We spent too much of our courtship in bars. That's when I discovered Eve had a drinking problem. *Nothing here that can't be handled,* I thought.

Our wedding was that August. For the first five years of our marriage, we lived in a small apartment in New York, had two children, Linda and Chet, and centered our activity about the young adult group. I learned quickly to keep Eve away from drinking occasions as much as possible.

After the birth of Chet, we found our apartment was too small for four so we moved into a house 75 miles north in the village of Carmel, New York. There Jeff was born. The main problem for me—a long commute to New York City.

The five most painful years of my life followed. To the outside world we were a normal Christian couple. Yet ours was an acutely dysfunctional home, with confused children trying to understand why Mommy was sick so often, and why Daddy had to work so much.

As a husband I was baffled by the insidious nature of alcoholism. It defied all logic. I sensed Eve was as helpless as I was. Once, near the breaking point, I went for a walk and kept repeating over and over, "The Lord is my Shepherd. I shall not want. . . ." To other pedestrians I must have looked like a babbling idiot. As Eve got progressively worse we steered her to a psychiatrist, then to Alcoholics Anonymous, then to a treatment center. She spent six months in a New York hospital. Nothing helped. Her father, a physician, had her hospitalized. Again to no avail. Years passed. Finally, a divorce was agreed upon with me receiving custody of the children.

Divorce is *defeat*—and *failure*. A defeat can be accepted fairly quickly. You bounce back. Seeing myself as a husband who failed took more time, for I was determined to blame the divorce on something else.

It took years, but finally I saw, accepted and repented of my failures as a husband. I had been faithful and a good provider, but I had my priorities wrong. They were:

> Work
> God and Family
> Recreation and Hobbies

As I have grown in faith and as a husband in two good marriages since then, my priorities now are:

> God
> Family
> Work
> Other

How do we men get so captured by our work that we become almost oblivious to the pain and anguish in our homes?

I have learned over the years that many men fall into this trap. We tend to become what we do well. The result—we can become so obsessed with our work that we make it our whole world to the exclusion of all else. During my marriage to Eve, I became totally absorbed in seeing *Guideposts* become a major publishing force. It eventually did. But I didn't know how to balance my life. I spent evenings in the office . . . I should have been at home. I carried my work home and was insensitive to what Eve was going through until it was too late.

If I knew back then what I know today about alcoholism, I am sure we could have helped Eve onto the recovery road. She is now living out her life in a wheelchair in a nursing home.

Painful admissions. But seeing and accepting my failure here enables me to say some things to my sons, Chet and Jeff, and to other husbands and potential husbands that I couldn't otherwise say.

1. *Husbands, your love for your wives is not complete unless you are willing to make sacrifices for them.*

When Paul compared the love of a husband for his wife to the way "Christ loved the church and gave Himself up for her" (Ephesians 5:25), he was telling a husband how to love. Sacrificial love means denying yourself to please your wife. It means giving up a favorite television program to take your wife shopping. It means turning down a golf game Saturday morning to visit your wife's relatives. It could mean giving up your life to save hers.

I am not saying that a husband should become a Caspar Milquetoast and relinquish his scripturally ordained role as spiritual head of his home. He should be ready to take strong moral positions and hold them. Christ took strong positions, but He gave Himself for His bride, the Church.

As a boy I was critical of my father because I thought he let my mother dominate our home. And when our father-son roles were reversed later in life he admitted he should have been stronger with her. Yet they loved each other for 56 years. When Dad died, Mother, supposedly the strong one, was lost without him.

97

The memories of my father that linger most vividly with me are examples of his patient, sacrificial spirit. When Mother came home sobbing after she had smashed up the car, Dad comforted her, put her to bed, gave her a sedative and arranged to have the car fixed. When Mother came home triumphant from a conference where she got a standing ovation as the main speaker, Dad set up a small homecoming party to celebrate. When Mother was near a nervous collapse while pregnant with my sister, Dad arranged for me as a seven-year-old to spend six months with relatives, took a short leave from his job at the university and personally saw her through the pregnancy and its aftermath.

Sacrificial love.

I didn't have it in my marriage to Eve and the marriage failed.

In my marriage to Catherine the testing time came early. We lived in Chappaqua, New York, forty minutes by train to the *Guideposts* office in New York City. Following a trip to Israel in 1963 Catherine developed a bronchial problem made more severe by her two-year bout with a lung infection in the 1940s. "Northern winters are hard on you," the doctor said. "Can you spend them in a warmer climate?"

I suggested that Catherine go to Florida for several weeks and find a place we could rent for the winter. She called me after several days in Delray Beach.

"Rentals are impossible to find," she reported, "but I have found the perfect house. Will you fly down and look at it?"

I did with deep misgivings. Buying a house in Florida made no economic sense unless . . . unless we moved there. What would that do to my position as a magazine editor, work I loved and had lost myself in?

I flew to Florida, agreed that the house was just right; and then came the painfully difficult decision that we should buy it, sell our house in Chappaqua and move to Florida. I now began commuting from south Florida to New York City every other week, which I did for ten years.

The marital sacrifice was difficult, but the move to Florida added years to Catherine's life. When I resigned from *Guideposts* in 1974, an opportunity opened up for a fulfilling second career in book publishing. Sacrifice has to work both ways if the marriage is to succeed. Catherine gave up a lot to be a mother to my three young children. When I see the fruits of this now in their lives and in their marriages, I am filled to overflowing with gratitude.

In my present marriage to Sandra, I am learning what it means to be a stepfather to three young people in their twenties (see chapter 7).

Most disturbing today is a trend by many young men who are not only unwilling to enter a marriage that calls for sacrifices, they are unwilling to marry at all. Their reasons:

- No need to marry to have regular safe sex. Find a woman who will agree to a living together arrangement.
- We don't want the responsibility and expense of children.
- Why get involved with emancipated, demanding wives?

Furthermore, the male reasoning goes, a live-in arrangement is the best way to prepare for marriage if, down the road, you do want to wed and have children.

Not so, say two University of Wisconsin researchers, Larry Bumpass and James Sweets. They recently did a study of couples who had lived together before they married to discover if such arrangements increased marriage stability. Using data from a 1987–89 federal survey, they compared a group of couples who lived together before marriage with a group of marrieds who had not. Over a ten-year period 38% of those who lived together before marriage had split up after being wed. Of the couples who had not lived together only 27% were later divorced.

I can certainly identify with these young men—and some not so young—who don't want to commit themselves to being a husband. Yet I feel sadness for them, too. They are shying away from one of the most basic truths of this life: *To get something good out of life you have to pour something of yourself into it.*

2. *A faithful husband stands out like an unblemished diamond, crystal clear and pure.*

This is the kind of statement I would like to see as a bumper sticker on a pick-up truck, or neatly printed on a company president's desk, or posted in the locker room of the world champion San Francisco Forty-Niners.

How do we come against the wave of articles, news reports, films and polls that say, in effect, adultery is acceptable behavior? Is this a campaign being waged by people who are simply trying to justify their own faithlessness?

On a recent Phil Donahue television program the famous talk show host interviewed a group of women on the subject of parental infidelity. In every case a daughter at a young age had discovered her father's adultery with another woman. In every case the results were devastating.

One teenager began using drugs.

Another became an alcoholic.

Another tried to commit suicide.

All had trouble trusting men from then on.

In each situation the family was ripped apart. Not all the marriages ended in divorce, but the trust level in each family was destroyed. In several families the generational pattern repeated itself: When the father was an adulterer, the son became one, too.

One mother in trying to explain it to her daughter said, "This is the way men are."

What an indictment!

In 1948 Alfred Kinsey shocked the world when he reported that fifty percent of American husbands had been unfaithful. In the early 1980s Shere Hite, in her study of the sexuality of 7,239 males, claimed that 72 percent of men married more than two years had cheated on their wives. More recent Gallup and Harris polls dispute these figures, claiming that many people tend to boast about their sexual activity when polled, while few brag about how virtuous they are.

Marriage forecasters, however, say that nearly two out of every three couples who marry today will end up in the divorce court tomorrow. A recent Cornell Medical College study disclosed that soon after marriage fifty percent of the couples began to wonder if their union would last.

Accurate figures about adultery are impossible to come by, but men always have and always will have to deal with the temptation to be unfaithful. A husband may have good intentions when he begins a marriage. When the intensity of the sexual relationship diminishes (as it always does), he begins to look at other women. At first it is out of curiosity. A small "blip" off the path of responsibility, as Dr. James Dobson calls it. "If he doesn't check his inclinations at that point," Dobson says, "the blip will become a bulge, and the illicit relationship will grow until it becomes a flaming passion."

A recent major book, *Men Who Can't Be Faithful*, listed ways a woman could keep her husband from being unfaithful. "Give sex a high priority" was stressed constantly. Also, "Watch your weight" . . . "Make yourself new to him" . . . "Bring back the art of seduction" . . . "Find new ways to be romantic" . . . and so on.

Helpful advice, I thought, *but somehow bland.* What was missing? Then it hit me. These points focused almost entirely on the physical relationship. What about the spiritual?

I read through the suggestions again. Not a single mention of anything spiritual. Nothing about faith or beliefs. No wonder they seemed lackluster.

A second thought struck. If bodily inducements are all the wife has in her repertoire of tricks to hold her man, the relationship is probably doomed. Gratifying a husband's physical needs is important, but this alone won't keep him from straying.

Some years ago when I worked in New York City, a group of us men met each Wednesday during lunch hour to eat sandwiches and talk in the board room of IBM's New York headquarters. Our objective—to find spiritual truth amid the tensions and pressures and confusions swirling about our everyday lives.

The eight of us who met Wednesdays were husbands.

One memorable day we got on the subject of whether fantasizing leads to adultery. Most of the dialogue was between two men whom I'll call Rod and Tom. Rod was quite open about himself. "I've always enjoyed fantasizing about other women," he said. "My wife, Sybil, has her fantasies, too. We know that as Christians we should not have adulterous relationships. But I think it is unrealistic to expect men not to think about sex with other women."

"Jesus has something to say about that," said Tom, a gentle, graying man with a regular twinkle in his eyes.

"I know the passage, too," replied Rod. "If I look at a woman lustfully, I've committed adultery with her. Sorry, but I can't buy it."

Tom looked thoughtful as he slowly unwrapped his sandwich. "It doesn't seem very reasonable, does it?"

"No, it isn't. It makes Jesus seem stern, austere, while I want to see Him as loving and understanding."

"But Rod, I see Jesus as both stern and loving, just the way I, as a father, try to be with my children."

It fascinated me how often our discussions seemed to come down to a sparring match between Rod and Tom. Rod was in his middle thirties, an emotional Latin type, mercurial, warmhearted, impulsive. Tom was ten years older, a thoughtful, careful man, gracious, sensitive.

"Do you feel guilty when you fantasize about another woman, Rod?" I asked.

"Well, yeah, sometimes."

"Do you feel guilty because of Sybil or because of Jesus' statement?"

Rod thought a moment. "The Bible passage implies that my thought of adultery is as bad as if I'd really gone to bed with another woman. That makes no sense. No one is hurt by my thought, although some people might get hurt if I act it out."

After a thoughtful silence, Tom picked up the discussion. "Jesus was not a woolly-thinking dreamer. He's not saying that there should be equal guilt for thought and action, only that the thought is the father of the deed, and that when you think about sleeping with another woman, you're committing adultery *in your heart*. The key here is these last three words."

"I'm not sure I really understand what you mean by a sexual fantasy," said one of the group.

Rod paused a moment and a gleam came into his eyes.

"There's all-out atomic war. Everything in the world is pretty much destroyed except this one plane flying in the South Pacific. I'm the pilot. In the plane are a dozen campus queens, girls who hired me to fly them to Australia. We have to land on a remote island. My job is to repopulate the earth with these good-looking young chicks."

There was silence for a while as all of us digested this mammoth ego trip. Tom was gazing out the window reflectively. "I think I ought to tell you men an experience I had with fantasy that was anything but harmless. My first marriage was filled with all kinds of problems, but Janet was a good kid even if she was a bit spoiled and immature. Like most couples, we both went into marriage expecting to get something special out of it and not thinking too much about what we had to give. When the sexual hang-ups came, as they always seem to, we talked about divorce. My ego was hurt because Janet lost her sense of excitement about sex. So I began fantasizing. With me, the thought was the father of the deed. I got involved with another woman in the office. That really tore it between Janet and me, and she divorced me."

"Are you saying that Christians should not have these fantasies?" asked Rod.

"I'm saying that my fantasizing was the first step toward adultery and the breakup of my marriage," Tom replied.

The meeting ended on that stark note as we all struggled with our own private thoughts.

3. *Husbands, the battle with temptations is always winnable when you get people praying for you.*

I wish I had known more about the power of intercession in my first marriage. There was so little prayer by us as a marriage team and for us. We knew almost nothing then about spiritual warfare.

When Catherine and I were married, we faced gigantic problems bringing two broken homes together. Impressed with her knowledge of Scripture and the beauty of her prayers, I made this suggestion:

"Catherine, why don't you take charge of the spiritual life of our family? You're a Bible scholar. Your prayers are beautiful. I'll handle things like family finances, keeping records, that sort of thing."

"I couldn't disagree with you more." Catherine's body quivered with intensity. "Len, I can't be the spiritual head of our home. It's unscriptural." Then she read me this passage from Ephesians: "Wives, submit to your husbands as to the Lord. For the husband is the head of the wife as Christ is the head of the church" (Ephesians 5:22–23, NIV).

I was surprised. This kind of submission was not what I expected from Catherine. It forced me to take spiritual leadership in our home. Soon we were rising an hour earlier to read Scripture and pray together.

There were so many prayer concerns I began writing them down on scraps of paper. Then I bought a notebook, which became a prayer log. In it I listed the prayers, by date, and the answers, by date. It became immensely valuable research. We were deep into intercession almost without knowing it.

One morning in 1979 Catherine had a personal encounter with the Lord during her prayer time. *You don't know enough about intercession,* He told her. Then He gave her a vision. First, she saw a vast sea of humanity with tremendous needs, which the Lord told her would increase in the years ahead. Second, she viewed another large group of people, young and old, men and women, from all nationalities, who had a special talent—they had been gifted with the desire to pray for others. Yet this gift was not being used. *You and Len search out these intercessors and get them praying for the needy,* came the Lord's instructions.

We obeyed. Today our prayer ministry called "Breakthrough" has over 2,500 intercessors enrolled to pray for the sick, the bereaved, the lonely and most of all hurting families. The result: We have been astonished and overwhelmed by the answers to prayer that have poured into our office.

The Lord, I have discovered, has a special heart for intercession. As a husband and father, I have also discovered how much I need people praying for me. When I face a difficult situation and ask others to pray for me I can almost feel the difference. When I allow a tempting thought to rest in my mind and then am flooded with remorse and contrition, someone is doubtless praying for my protection.

If as a husband you are estranged from your wife, or are confused, hurting, angry, rebellious or tempted toward wrong behavior, seek out intercessors in a nearby church or write for prayer to Breakthrough (Lincoln, Virginia 22078).

4. *Husbands, accept the fact that you are under attack by forces you cannot see, that you have a very real enemy in Satan who wants to destroy your marriage.*

The fact that a dark force out there wants to break up your marriage should arouse your fighting spirit. "How dare he single me out!" Your home suddenly becomes a place you will go all-out to protect.

As a husband you need to understand exactly what spiritual warfare is. This is not difficult. There are many books on the subject. More and more churches are dealing with it.

Most important for every husband is to accept the authority the Lord gives him when he becomes the spiritual head of his home.

With this authority a husband can pray against the dark forces he may feel pressing in on him and his family. He prays this way against sickness, against temptations, against forces in his community that would corrupt his children. The prayer for his home could go like this:

Lord, with the authority You gave me as the head of this household, I come against all perverse spirits, against principalities and the forces of darkness that are trying to upset the peace and order of our home. In the name of Jesus I rebuke these spirits and cast them out. They have no ground in this house. I pray now that You would fill this place with Your Spirit, Your love, Your peace, Your joy.

Hearing Peter Wagner, a professor at Fuller Theological Seminary, spell out how the enemy works was chilling. In this country there is a tremendous increase of Satanists who are committed *to pray to Satan for the breakup of Christian marriages, to pray that husbands will succumb to adultery.* Satanists single out certain communities where influential men are living to pray this negative prayer. Satanic churches meanwhile are springing up everywhere.

As a husband I have been involved in spiritual warfare now for years. During this time I have accumulated in my arsenal some special Scriptures that are real weapons against the enemy. Here's one that helps me deal with wrong thinking:

> For the weapons of our warfare are not carnal, but mighty through God to the pulling down of strongholds . . . bringing into captivity every thought to the obedience of Christ.
>
> 2 Corinthians 10:4–5, KJV

For an aggressive defense:

> Resist the devil, and he will flee from you.
>
> James 4:7, KJV

For protection:

> He [God] will shield you with his wings! They will shelter you. His faithful promises are your armor.
>
> Psalm 91:4, LB

Coping with fears:

> The Lord is my helper, and I will not fear what man
> shall do unto me.
>
> Hebrews 13:6, KJV

Here's the way I prepare every day for battle with dark
forces:

> Put on the full armor of God so that you can take
> your stand against the devil's schemes . . .
> . . . with the belt of truth buckled around your waist
> . . . with the breastplate of righteousness in place
> . . . with your feet fitted with the readiness that
> comes from the gospel of peace
> . . . with the shield of faith in position
> . . . with the helmet of salvation on your head
> . . . with the sword of the Word in your hand.
>
> Ephesians 6:11–17, paraphrase

Ed Cole, president of Manhood, Inc., is a prayer warrior
who speaks with a prophetic voice to the men of today.
His ministry, along with a few others, forms the nucleus
of a group of revitalized men who battle Satan every day
as they spearhead the coming of new moral leadership
into the world.

At a recent men's conference I attended, with many
husbands present, Ed stood before us and opened with
prayer. Then God suddenly empowered him and he thun-
dered: "If some of you here today are committing adultery, fornication, homosexuality, incest, or habitual
masturbation; indulging in pornography; gratifying your-
selves with sexual fantasies or any other kind of sex sin; I

command you in the name of Jesus Christ to repent and be restored to a right relationship with God the Father."

As the words cut through the air like an electric shock, the room fell silent for a split second. Then with a single explosive motion, hands shot into the air and men began crying out in praise and worship to God. Deep inside they had longed to be shocked out of their sinful natures. They had hungered for God's voice to touch their lives.

Ed Cole didn't seem surprised by the men's reaction that day as they swarmed forward for prayer and ministry. "I have watched God's power change men at these meetings. I have literally seen them grow in spirit before my eyes. It's awesome," he said later.

5. *Husbands, renew the vows you and your wife said at your wedding. Find a time and place to repeat them at regular intervals.*

I met Sandy in August 1984, a year and a half after Catherine's death. Her joyous spirit and love of the Lord drew me to her.

At our wedding I said these words to her: "I, Leonard, pledge to you, Sandy, that I will be faithful to you . . . for better or for worse, whether rich or poor, in sickness and in health, until death do us part." She in turn made this pledge to me.

Today we have Communion together on occasions when we feel under attack, or in disagreement, or full of gratitude. We kneel, serve each other the elements—"The body of Christ broken for you . . . the blood of the Lord shed for you"—then while holding hands we repeat the vows made at our wedding.

If there are any barriers separating us, they dissolve as we focus on the Lord who is our strength.

Over the years I have learned that if I am fully to love my wife, there is so much more to it than the sex act. It begins in the morning with touch, soft words and tenderness. While praying together, we hold hands. Tensions disappear as we love each other while we worship God.

Hugs are hugely important to Sandy. Several prepare us for the separation of daily work. From my desk I call to say, "I love you."

In the evening we can always find time for a short date, even if it is drinking a cup of coffee together in the living room after dinner, or holding hands as we go outside for an evening walk. This is our talk time . . . to catch up on the day's news . . . to share the small triumphs and failures.

And to laugh. No day is ever complete unless there are some good laughs. We find them in our description of events and places . . . in the dumb things we do or say . . . in the nicknames we make up for each other. The glue that brings deep satisfaction to a marriage is not sex, but this kind of companionship.

Always there is touch . . . holding hands . . . massaging backs . . . stealing kisses . . . rubbing noses . . . and hugs. At least ten hugs a day.

It was Sandy who suggested the visit to Eve. "She was your wife for nine years, Len, and the mother of your children. There's bound to be a lot of unhealed grief and pain."

Everything in me resisted this suggestion. You want to remove yourself as far as possible from a failure in your life. Eve and I had kept in touch through letters and phone calls; I had maintained support payments to her; the children had been loving, making occasional visits to the nursing home in the Midwest where Eve resided; but I had not seen her in thirty years.

Then came the call from Linda. She was taking her one-year-old daughter, my granddaughter, to visit Eve. I heard myself say, "I'll go with you."

When we arrived at the nursing home, Eve was sitting in her wheelchair finishing breakfast. Her body was ailing, but her face was alive, her eyes warm. The meeting was awkward at first, but not for long. Soon we were going back thirty years to reminisce over the good times we had had together.

There was no trace of bitterness in Eve, only gratitude. Gratitude that Catherine had been such a good mother to her children. (In fact, Eve had written to Catherine to express this.) Gratitude that her children had visited her in their adult years. Gratitude that her material needs had been provided for. I was astonished. Eve was blessing us.

We all went to church together and met Eve's friends; in fact, Linda and I were asked to stand and be introduced publicly during the service. It was a dramatic moment, as though we were acknowledging before the world our responsibility for our relationships and giving testimony to God's unlimited power to heal. Before our departure, the three of us held hands and prayed together while baby Whitaker played on the floor beside us. The healing tears flowed as we asked forgiveness for the hurts each one of us had brought on the others.

Later I reflected: Try as he may, a husband can never

just end the relationship with the mother of his children. It can fester or it can be healed, but it is eternal.

Questions for Reflection

1) Do you see your marriage as a partnership with God at the center? If you are single would you want this kind of marriage?
2) What are the priorities in your life? Are they different from those of your spouse or girlfriend?
3) What is your evaluation of the sexual revolution?
4) Do you agree that fantasizing about sex can lead to adultery? If so, how do you stop it?
5) What does it mean to honor, cherish and love your wife?

6
Father

Fathers, provoke not your children to wrath.

Ephesians 6:4, KJV

As we move into the 1990s, a deeply disturbing situation faces us in the United States—in fact, worldwide. Fathers by the millions are saying to their families, "I quit. I'm leaving. You're on your own."

The statistics are devastating:

* Close to two million divorced or separated fathers are refusing to pay court-ordered child support, amounting to $3.7 billion each year.

* Studies show that a father's absence from the home creates the climate for his children to have (a) a higher delinquency rate, (b) more premarital pregnancies, (c) lower school performance, (d) greater drug use, (e) greater tendency toward crime.

The fact is that being a good father today tests manhood as never before. A father has to work harder to support his family; he needs to know more about the machines and computers that make his home function; he must deny himself more because there are so many more options for self-realization than fifty years ago; he has to show more patience and understanding to cope with additional pressures on his wife and children; and somehow he must acquire the wisdom of Solomon to resolve conflicts in his home. All this on top of being a good husband to a wife who is probably working part-time or full-time and thus is heavily overburdened herself.

So it is not surprising that so many men are deciding in large numbers either not to marry or, if they do marry, not to have children, or if they do have children, to leave.

Yet the situation today is not all bad. A new breed of males is emerging that is throwing off the shackles of narcissism, playboyism, selfism, alcohol and drug dependency to become responsible fathers. They are playing more with their children. They are changing diapers and being full-time partners as parents in ways my generation rarely did. They are rising early in the morning to pray with their wives. They are becoming "spiritual heads" of their homes.

All this means that more and more fathers are saying "not me" to that negative picture of themselves as incompetent, bumbling parents whose only legitimate territory is the office or factory. They are going back to basics, to Scripture, to chart their new course.

The Fatherhood of God

Strength in fatherhood begins with knowing the Father in heaven. Since we all are creations of this Father, the way we picture Him is important. If we see Him as loving,

115

understanding, but firm with us, we will tend to be this way as fathers to our children.

Children's concepts of God tend to parallel their views of their fathers. Any child who has a mean and irresponsible earthly father is likely to hold that image of the heavenly Father. If a child grows up without a father, he may conclude there is no God at all.

Psychologists say that most people today have three basic problems: the problems of identity, security and self-worth. All these can be resolved when we know God as our Father. As a son of God the Father I have an identity. Since His Word says that the heavenly Father is "my refuge and fortress" (Psalm 91), then He is my security. My self-worth grows and strengthens as I learn that my Father in heaven really loves me, yes, even small, insignificant me.

Derek Prince tells the story of a troubled woman who stopped him on the way to an engagement. He listened to her for a minute or so, sensed her low self-worth and had her pray this prayer: "God, I thank You that You love me, that You are my Father, that I am Your child, that I am not rejected or unwanted or inferior. I thank You that I belong to You, that I belong to the best family in the universe. I accept Your love for me and I love You, Father."

Derek had to rush on to his engagement. A month or so later he got a letter from the woman in which she described how this new concept of having her very own Father in heaven and belonging to the best family in the universe had revolutionized her life.

For years I have heard preachers and teachers urge men to be a people set apart for God and thus become part of "the priesthood of all believers." This is not easy for men, yet I'm convinced that the spiritual health of a church today depends on laymen taking on priestly functions. During His ministry on earth Jesus was Prophet, Priest and King to His followers, and challenged them to do the things He did.

In this sense fathers need to be prophets, priests and kings in their own homes. Let's see how it can work:

The Father as Prophet

The dictionary definition of a prophet: "A person who speaks for God, or by divine inspiration." Moses was a great prophet. He sought God's counsel and passed His instructions and commandments on to the chosen people.

I can hear the chorus of fathers saying, "Well, I'm no Moses." I would be among them. In my first marriage I was a most uninspired prophet. When the marriage failed and I found myself a single parent rearing three small children, the procession of housekeepers began. Six in a period of eighteen months. Linda became a surrogate mommy at age ten, did a remarkable job with her two smaller brothers, helping them get dressed, feeding them breakfast in front of the television set (usually orange juice and doughnuts).

On weekends I took over household responsibilities. Hamburgers, hot dogs and fried chicken (cooked by the housekeeper Friday afternoon) were standard fare. On special occasions, steak. If I accidentally flipped a hamburger onto the floor, no problem. Just put it back in the skillet and cook out any impurities. Never any complaints.

As a single parent I discovered that commuting to a

demanding job 75 miles away and keeping order in the home took all my time and energy. In a situation like that there is almost no time to think or plan or socialize. You exist day by day, concerned only with survival. I did pray for help, for a mate, and this prayer was marvelously answered in Catherine.

My education as "prophet and spiritual head of the home" began at this point. Twelve years as editor of *Guideposts* had given me a base of knowledge, but there is a big difference between head knowledge and day-by-day application. In the weeks that followed as spiritual head I instigated:

1) *A prayer log* during Catherine and my early morning devotional time in which I recorded our needs and concerns.

2) *Family devotions* right after the evening meal (Scripture reading, sharing, prayers). The children learned to pray out loud.

3) *Story times.* Children love stories, especially ones about adventure, and just before they go to bed. Mine involved a hero I named "Lucky" (I would give him a different name today). Lucky was a freelance reporter who was always where the action was. He was a Good Samaritan who rescued people from burning buildings, from sinking boats, from man-eating sharks. He did it through the power of prayer.

Whether he was hanging by one pinkie over a nest of poisonous snakes, or tied upside-down over a boiling pot by an African tribe, or buried alive in a snow avalanche, or kidnapped by the Mafia, through hearing the voice of God Lucky found the way out. Instruction in how to pray and have faith was woven into each story and each story always ended with a cliffhanger—to be continued the next bedtime.

In this second marriage it did not take me long to find the Scripture passage upon which I was to base my role as prophet. The sixth chapter of Ephesians, verse four: *"Fathers, provoke not your children to wrath: but bring them up in the nurture and admonition of the Lord"* (KJV).

Two words became the cornerstone of Catherine and my approach: *nurture* and *admonition*. We saw nurture as meaning proper teaching; admonition as meaning firm discipline.

An episode with Chester, age nine, tested me as a father. On a shopping trip Chester slipped three candy bars into his pocket unnoticed. The evidence turned up in his room later—three candy bar wrappers in the wastebasket. When confronted, he admitted the theft.

As prophet to the family I had to speak for God as I administered punishment. How to do this? Then it came to me. Read and discuss the Ten Commandments during our after-dinner family time.

I did this, explaining how each Commandment was relevant to today. At bedtime I went up to my son's room. He was sitting on the bed, expecting me. I sat down beside him.

"I'm sorry I stole those candy bars, Dad," he said, a stricken look in his large brown eyes.

119

I put my arm around him. "When you violate one of God's commandments, son, there are three things you need to do. Do you know what they are?"

He shook his head.

"The first is to admit your wrongdoing. You did that this afternoon. The second is to say you're sorry. You did that just now. There's one more step. Do you know what it is?"

"Never do it again," he said hopefully.

"I certainly hope you don't," I replied. "But the third step is to make restitution. Return the money and tell the store clerk you're sorry."

"You mean I have to go back to the store?"

"That's right. First thing in the morning. I'll advance you the money from next week's allowance."

Chet was white-faced the following day when we parked in front of the store. "Will you come inside with me, Daddy?"

"No. This is something you have to do all by yourself."

More anguished looks with those contrite brown eyes. Slowly he opened the car door and walked into the store, the coins clutched in his hand. My heart ached for him. Five minutes later he came out and climbed back into the car.

"Well, what happened?"

"She took the money and patted me on the head. She said it was nice, but not necessary."

Inwardly, I groaned. Why are people such "panty-waists" in situations like this? "You understand why it was necessary, don't you, son?"

He nodded, sighed and leaned back against the seat.

At a recent family get-together, Chester, now a father

himself, reminded me of the candy-stealing episode 25 years before. "Going into that store and admitting I was a thief was one of the most painful moments of my life," he said. "But you'll be happy to know, Dad, that the memory of it was seared on my mind forever. Not once since then was I ever tempted to shoplift."

Fathers who are inclined to be easygoing in disciplining children need to read about Eli, a priest of the Israelites, who ministered properly to the people but did not discipline his sons, Hophni and Phinehas. As a result, Eli's sons became so immoral that the Lord intervened directly, saying that He would judge and punish Eli's house forever, for his sons were blaspheming God, and *"Eli did not restrain them"* (1 Samuel 3:13).

How this speaks to the busy father who puts his calling, no matter how noble, above his responsibilities as a parent! I have already confessed my sin of putting work ahead of family. I also had a tendency to dismiss what I considered to be minor shortcomings of my sons by saying, "Boys will be boys." Catherine, in the role of loving critic, called me on this.

The Father as Priest

A priest "performs religious rites, makes sacrificial offerings for his flock," says the dictionary.

So if the father acts as a priest, he does all this by leading his family in worship and "making offerings" of intercession, praise and thanksgiving for his children.

How does he do this in a practical way?

One way is to get up early in the morning to pray for his family.

121

I did this regularly during my marriage to Catherine . . . with her when we were both home, by myself when alone. After Catherine's death in 1983, there followed a two-year period when I faltered somewhat in my prayer life. With marriage to Sandy my father responsibilities increased.

Every morning Sandy and I pray for the three children of my first marriage, Linda, Chet and Jeff . . . my stepson, Peter John Marshall . . . all four of their spouses, Phil, Susan, Nancy and Edith . . . my four grandchildren, Jacob, Hadley, Mary Catherine and Whitaker . . . my three step-grandchildren, Mary, Peter Jonathan and David Marshall . . . my three stepchildren by my wife, Sandy: Brad, Brent and Lisa . . . Sandy's mother, Elizabeth, and her father and stepmother, Richard and Nora.

The others we pray for in our family bring the total up to 52. Since I have trouble keeping names straight, this kind of prayer is an excellent memory booster.

"Do you pray for them all every day by name?" we were asked once after a prayer workshop.

"Yes, every day. Over a year, it's true, we may miss a few days because of travel complications. After each year we evaluate the lives of each person prayed for. Changes for the better in terms of health and faith growth have been significant. Sandy and I believe that *praying for all family members by name is the single most important thing we can do for them.*"

God honors the father who takes seriously the priestly position of protector of his family. Remember the father who had heard of Christ's miracles and brought his son to Him for healing? "Teacher," he said, "my son is possessed by a spirit. . . . It throws him to the ground. He foams at the mouth, gnashes his teeth and becomes raged."

"Bring the boy to Me," said Jesus.

The moment the father led his son to Jesus, the boy went into a convulsion and fell to the ground.

"How long has he been like this?" Jesus asked his father.

"From childhood. If You can do anything, take pity on us and help us."

"If I can?" said Jesus. "Everything is possible for him who believes."

"I do believe," the father replied. "Help my unbelief."

Jesus must have loved this man's honesty and father's heart. He rebuked the spirit, which came out shrieking. The boy fell on the ground as if dead until Jesus took him by the hand and lifted him to his feet, healed. (See Mark 9:14–29.)

Jesus is saying something important here: *Fathers, believe for your children. Fathers, believe for your grandchildren.*

The Lord honors and blesses the father who will intercede and "stand in the gap," believing for his family. Sometimes God will move a father into a position in which he must acknowledge his faith above the faith of any other person in the vicinity.

Over the years I have learned to be a priest to my family in connection with travel, for we are a family constantly on the move either by auto or plane. The prayer in each situation is very specific. In September 1969, for example, Catherine, Chet, Jeff and I began a trip from her mother's home in Virginia to our Florida home. Before leaving, I said this prayer: "By authority of my position as spiritual head of this family, I ask for Your protection of us as we drive south. I also ask, Lord, that You send angels 'to ride shotgun' on the hood of our car to protect us on this trip until we are safe at home."

No one in our family snickers over that kind of prayer anymore, especially after this particular trip. We arrived at our Florida residence safely. It was a steamy hot day. Usually after such a trip the boys jumped into the pool for a swim. This time for some reason they did not.

That night when I turned the switch that lit the pool, nothing happened. I looked more closely. The switch had been "on" all the time. My heart did a quick flip-flop.

The light had shorted. How would that happen? By water leaking into the pool light. If that was true the whole pool was electrified!

White-faced, I turned off the switch. Taped it over. Called the electrician. When he came the next day, he confirmed my worst fears. "It's a good thing none of you went swimming with the switch on," he said. "We've had so many deaths here in Florida from people jumping into electrified pools that they've passed new legislation against installing any pool lights without strong safeguards."

Now it was time for a father's thanksgiving. Gathering the family together, I praised God not only for His protection of us during our trip, but also for covering Chet and Jeff so that they didn't jump into the pool after we arrived home.

Sometimes the results of a father's priestly role are visible to all, as in the pool episode. Most of the time we praying fathers never know when or how God's protection and ministry to our families occur. But they do occur.

The Father as King

The guideline for the father as king is 1 Timothy 3:2–4: The "overseer [father] . . . must manage his own family well and see that his children obey him with proper respect" (NIV).

What does a king do? He rules. What does a father do as head of his home? He rules.

"Now wait a minute," says the wife. "I thought marriage was to be like a triangle! God at the top, husband and wife at the corners, equal partners."

That's right—being equal partners in the day-by-day family life is important. For we all know horror stories of tyrannical husbands and fathers who dominate wives and alienate children. That's why husband and wife need to operate as a team. But every team needs a captain to make decisions under special circumstances.

What kinds of circumstances?

What if the husband feels he should change jobs and move to a new location—but the wife disagrees? Does she have veto power? What if teenage children too big for the mother to handle refuse to obey her? Does the father just ignore this defiance? What if husband and wife can't agree on where to attend church? Does this mean they just don't go? What if the father wants his son to attend Sunday school and the mother doesn't? Does the boy stay home? Since decisions must be made almost daily, the father exercises his ruling power.

What about situations when the husband-father is not a believer and the wife is? What happens when she wants to take their child to church and he resists?

In situations when the father is *not* committed to the Lord, he is *not* prepared to be prophet, priest and king to his family. He has rejected his role as head of his family and thus does not have an anointing from God. The wife in such situations has no choice but to assume spiritual leadership. Her daily prayer should be that her husband will see how rudderless he and the family are and seek God as the answer. If he becomes one of the millions of "dropout" fathers, or renegade husbands, the chances are that another marriage will go to the divorce court.

In his book *Mere Christianity*, C. S. Lewis went into the question of headship, stating that an attempt at total equality between husbands and wives always breaks down when there is a sharp disagreement. "They can't decide by a majority vote, can they?" Then Lewis continues as follows:

> . . . Is there any serious feeling that the head should be the woman? . . . Even a woman who wants to be head of her own house does not usually admire the same state of things when she finds it going on next door. She is much more likely to say, "Poor Mr. X! Why he allows that appalling woman to boss him about the way she does is more than I can imagine." I do not think she is even very flattered if anyone mentions the fact of her own "headship." There must be something unnatural about the rule of wives over husbands, because the wives themselves are half ashamed of it and despise the husbands whom they rule.

Thank God there is a trend today for us fathers to assume headship roles in the family. We are going to make mistakes. We are going to need support and encouragement from our wives and, yes, correction. Husbands and wives desperately need an understanding that when correction is needed by either, it should be done in love. But it should be done!

In my marriage to Catherine she encouraged me to be prophet, priest and king of the family. But she reserved the right to take the position of "loyal opposition" in any disagreements. And there were plenty.

When we had a crisis with Linda and her failing grades at college, I was amused at how quickly Catherine looked to me to take charge.

Linda had attended a girls' preparatory school, living away from home through all four years of high school. She then planned to attend Duke University. That summer our family gathered for a week of "family time" and great strides were made in all our relationships, especially between Linda and Catherine. Eager for more time with the family, Linda decided to live at home and commute to a nearby college for her freshman year. She did well in that school, but regretted the lack of much social life. For her sophomore year Linda chose to go to Ohio Wesleyan. It was her first time away from home in an unstructured situation. The freedom was too much for her. She chose to socialize, to get involved in student activities, to date every night, anything but study.

When it was time for Linda to come home for Christmas, she admitted she was late getting term papers done in all of her courses. "Better stay there until you finish them," I suggested. She agreed.

Four days before Christmas I called again. "Have you finished the papers?"

"No." There was a stubborn note in her voice.

"How far along are you?"

"Not very far."

Long silence. A series of episodes flicked across my mind of her testing us again and again.

"You obviously do not want to stay in college, Linda. Pack up all your things and come home," I said grimly.

In our prayer time the next morning, Catherine agreed with me that a tough front was needed with Linda. When she arrived home, we greeted her lovingly, said nothing at first about her late papers. The day after Christmas, we sat down for a talk. I studied my daughter with deep inner anguish. To this father, her long hair, wire-rimmed glasses and impassive expression typified the student of the late 1960s. Linda had the brains and talent to do whatever she wanted with her life. The desire was lacking.

"Linda, what do you want to do with your life?" I began.

She stared at me. "What do you mean?"

"I mean your future, beginning the first of next year. You can't go back to college because of your grades. So let's talk about what you're going to do in the world."

"I flunked just one course. I'll get a C in one, the rest are incomplete," she said.

"With your poor study habits I doubt if the college officials will let you back in school. We certainly won't pay for an education that means so little to you," I replied. "So let's talk about what kind of work you can do."

Then I explained that our Florida community had few job opportunities, suggested several other locations, named contacts she could make, outlined a plan she could follow. "You might get a job as a receptionist, file clerk or typist. I'll pay your travel to any city you select, plus your living expenses at the YWCA until you find a job."

"Are you saying, Dad, that if I flunk out of school, I can't come back home and live?"

"Yes, Linda. This is not the right place for you to start a new life."

As my daughter stared at me coldly, my heart was breaking. I felt like a cruel monarch, sending my charge out into the cold world.

Early the next morning I heard the typewriter pounding away. Linda emerged only for quick bites of food. All day long she worked. And the next. When I asked what she was doing, Linda replied tersely, "My college papers."

Several days later she called the dean of students at Ohio Wesleyan. Then she reported back to me, very businesslike. "I've finished all but one of my papers," she said. "That one is too late anyway. I've already failed the course."

"What did the dean say?" I asked.

"He will take my case up with the academic board and call me back," she replied.

When the call came from the dean, Linda listened quietly, took some notes, said thank-you and hung up.

"The dean says that since I've written the papers and seem to want to work, they will let me come back on a probation basis," she reported. "But I have to get a *B* average the rest of this year or they won't let me go into the junior class. Is this okay with you?"

With a deep sense of relief, I agreed.

The change in Linda's attitude that next year was dramatic. She finished with *A*'s and *B*'s—easily meeting the *B*-average requirement. When she was graduated from Ohio Wesleyan in 1971 Linda was the fourth-generation LeSourd to walk forward and receive that diploma over a series of thirty-year intervals. My grandfather, Marion Le-Sourd, was of the class of 1881; his son, Howard, was graduated in 1911; I was in the class of 1941; and now—again, exactly thirty years later—Linda in the class of 1971. Not only Catherine and I, but my father and mother, too, flew out for the special occasion.

In that situation with Linda I had acted as the ruling parent. But I had prayed for and received God's guidance, sought and received my wife's support. If I had been too autocratic, I could have alienated my daughter; if I had been too soft, I would have drawn Linda's contempt. There are times like this when the head of the home must rule, painful as it is.

The Family Tree

When a man accepts his position as head of the family, he will become a better father if he knows his family tree. He should go back at least to his great-grandfather and chart all the branches down to his own family and children. Were there serious illnesses? Did they continue in future generations? Was there any alcoholism? Divorce? Mental problems? What about the generational effect? The father will discover that Exodus 20:5—the sins of the fathers are visited on their children to the third and fourth generations—is almost always borne out.

Before doing a workshop with Sandy on compulsive-addictive behavior several years ago, I put together my family tree to see how the pattern worked out with five generations of LeSourd men. I began with my grandfather. He was a preacher, lived to age 94, a frugal man, good father, solid all the way.

My father was a preacher for almost ten years until he switched to education; he ended up, as I have said, as dean of the School of Communications at Boston University. He was beloved by all, a good father, a faithful husband, a solid citizen, until his death at 82.

How fortunate I, the third generation, am to have this heritage! For reasons I am still trying to understand, I rebelled against my heritage until age 29 when I settled down to become a writer, editor, publisher. Despite a failed marriage, I held true to my generational pattern of conscientious fatherhood with my three children.

The fourth generation of men: my two sons, Chet and Jeff. Both are married, Christians. Chet and his wife, Susan, have a nine-year-old son and a six-year-old daughter. Chet is an excellent father. Jeff and his wife, Nancy, are newly married, now expecting their first child. Jeff has all the attributes of the ideal father.

Fifth generation: Jacob LeSourd, at nine, already shows evidence of his lineage: athletic ability, spiritual leadership, a caring heart, potential to be a good father.

As I report these facts I feel an overwhelming sense of gratitude to God for His mercy and patience with me. The truth is—I nearly destroyed the generational pattern through my rebellion and willfulness. The turnaround came with my encounter with the living Lord at the Ramapo retreat center.

I didn't realize at the time how tremendous the stakes were for the future of our branch of the LeSourd family. It was as if the Lord was saying to me, *You have lived for yourself for 29 years. What have you accomplished? Your achievements have glorified you and you alone. The path that you are on leads to despair and death. Heed My call on your life and I will give you a new direction to travel and a fruitful life.*

Always we have freedom of choice. I could have declined His invitation. The warfare inside me was intense, but I chose life, not death.

Some who do their family trees will be dismayed to see that the curse of alcoholism, or adultery, or divorce, or physical infirmity has plagued the family for generation after generation. Despair will often result unless action is taken. The curses on any family can be broken.

The necessary action can go in several directions. Seek a Christian counselor or pastor who understands the generational problem and who knows how to break the curses through prayer. The bondage can also be broken in a family get-together when the father will take on the mantle of authority God has given him and will go through a procedure like this:

First all family members gathered together need to be in agreement: (a) that they belong to the Lord, (b) that the generational bondage (whatever it is) needs to be broken, (c) that the father figure is to take authority as "head" of the family and lead the prayer.

Second, there should be a time for confession and repentance of anything relating to the generational sin being dealt with. Everyone present needs to be open and vulnerable regarding his or her spiritual state.

Third, prayer and laying-on-of-hands should follow for each person involved. For example, the prayer for a father who needs to be severed from the alcoholism curse of his parents could go like this:

"Lord, we are gathered here to break the family curse of alcohol that has plagued this family for many years. As a family we kneel before You and repent of our sinfulness. We repent of our indifference to Your commandments. We repent of our sloth, our unforgiveness, our lack of faith, our prayerlessness. Now, Lord, we lay our hands upon this father and ask that You heal and deliver him from his bondage to the alcohol curse in his family. In the name of Jesus we come against this stronghold of alcohol. We rebuke Satan. We bind him and place him at the foot of the cross. We now cut the tie between this father and his addiction to alcohol forever. We sever the cord that has kept all other men in this family in bondage. We declare now that from this date and forevermore our family will be free of this curse. We invite the Holy Sprit to enter 'our house' and fill us all with His love and joy and power so that our lives will bear good fruit to all succeeding generations. In the name of Jesus we make this prayer."

Questions for Reflection

1) If you have a problem with your earthly father, has this affected your ability to love and honor your heavenly Father?
2) As a father how many times have you spoken for God as prophet to your family?
3) How do you see the priestly role of a father being different from that of a prophet?
4) Does it bother you to try to be a king to your family?
5) What problems do you see in making out your family tree?

7
Stepfather

Count it all joy when you fall into various trials, knowing that the testing of your faith produces patience.

James 1:2–3, NKJ

At age 27 Lisa said she knew exactly what she was doing when she decided to live with her boyfriend. She loved him but said she was not ready to consider marriage now, perhaps never.

Sandy, her mother, and I, her stepfather, were concerned about Lisa's decision. We felt it was not only wrong, but that Lisa would end up being hurt. We envisioned this lovely young auburn-haired woman marrying a mature, loving man and having beautiful children. When Sandy voiced these feelings to her, Lisa responded with a trace of amusement in her voice.

"If I love a man and don't want to get married, what am I to do?"

"Wait."

"Wait for what?"

"Until you are ready to get married."

"Mom, no one does that anymore. Furthermore, I don't

have marriage as my goal in life. Most marriages I have seen have ended up in divorce. Or the home situation is so bad, there should be a divorce. Who needs all that?"

Devastating! As a child, Lisa had witnessed her parents' deep unhappiness, seen her mother go through the trauma of alcoholism and two divorces. Nor was Lisa's experience unique. As Sandy reviewed all of Lisa's friends over the past years, she discovered that, yes, Lisa had been right. Most came from broken homes.

We were further jolted recently by a neighbor's disclosure that her daughter had come home from junior high school one day somewhat embarrassed by the fact that she was the only girl in her crowd who had *just one father and one mother.* "All my friends talk about their different mothers and fathers. They look at me as sort of an oddball," she said.

As Lisa's stepfather for the past five years, I often wondered what my role should be in her life. Since she lived across the country several thousand miles away, there were few opportunities to talk face to face. At Christmas we usually had a father-daughter lunch, occasions to get acquainted more than opportunities for deep sharing. Always I found my heart deeply touched by a wistful quality in her. She truly wanted to trust me, to bask in a father's love.

How could I bring this about?

As Sandy and I discussed this situation one night, I studied my wife. Though her face was concerned and there were lines on her forehead, she looked ten years younger than her 53 years. Her hair, tinted blonde when I first met her, was now a natural salt-and-pepper gray. "In my recovery I'm discovering how important it is to be the person I really am—that includes hair and all," Sandy had decided.

"Each year you grow younger," my children told me at a recent family gathering. "How do you do it?" In reply I pointed to Sandy.

When Sandy entered my life she infused me with a new dimension of joy and love. She also brought me into the present from the past, acquainting me with a whole new world of people imprisoned by drugs and alcohol and a newly named condition for an age-old problem called co-dependency.

As I edited her book *The Compulsive Woman*, a deep look into her own life of compulsive/addictive behavior, I encountered terms and phrases I never knew before: In addition to co-dependency there was dry drunk, intervention, adult children of alcoholics (ACOAs), Twelve-step programs, dysfunctional family. Two years after we were married, we were doing workshops on the subject "Victory Over Self-Defeating Lifestyles." I could hardly believe the words coming out of my mouth as I described my own co-dependency (resulting from my first marriage) and my workaholism, which I had admitted reluctantly. I had even discovered to my dismay that I fitted the description of a sportsaholic. The large crowds flocking to these workshops surprised me. So many people are eager to be freed from various bondages.

Coming from a severely dysfunctional family, it was no wonder that Lisa was cynical about marriage. I wrote her a long letter. Here are excerpts:

What bothers me most about your live-in relation-ship is that men have all the advantages in these situations. When it ends, they go blithely to their next adventure while women usually lick their wounds and try to pick up the pieces of their lives. It is all so one-sided.

I have watched how men handle these situations. With cold hearts they take what they want and then leave when they are tired or bored. Women work harder to keep the relationships going, to try to please the man, to try to build a home situation that is solid and stable. Because they have these nesting qualities women are bruised and hurt so much more easily than men.

I think you are a very special woman, Lisa. You have beauty and you have grace. You have much to offer a man. My hope and dream for you, Lisa, is that you will meet the man who has high ideals and who wants a solid and long-lasting relationship with just one woman—in a marriage situation.

Sandy and I are having a wonderful marriage together because we have learned the hard way. God is now our boss. Through prayer we can go to Him and get answers to our problems. He guides us, He sustains us, He protects us, He loves us. He gives excitement to our lives that we have never found on our own.

I am sure you will think this is a very preachy letter, Lisa, yet it does come from my heart. I love you. I want the best for you.

Lisa thanked me for the letter. She knew I had written it out of love and this touched her. Changes are taking place in her life. In a recent letter she said, "I pray about my situation here every day and wonder if this is where the Lord wants me."

Both of Lisa's brothers—Brad, 29, and Brent, 28—had viewed me warily from the beginning, determined to be loyal to their father. Their reticence said to me: "Our mother loves you and that's fine. We know you're religious, like Mom, and that's fine, too, but don't push it on us. We want to go our own way."

The first time I met Brad I was alone in the home of Sandy's friend Marge Switzer, where we were staying during a visit to Billings, Montana. As we sat down in the living room, I asked him if he had a goal in life. He looked uncomfortable. "What would you like to be five years from now?" I tried.

"An airline pilot," he replied.

At last—common ground. For the next ten minutes until Sandy arrived, we talked about flying, comparing the planes of today with those I flew back in World War II.

Brent was a salesman for high-tech sound equipment. In talking with him I discovered that his heart's desire was to compose music.

The Key Is Patience

Being a stepfather to adult children is difficult. A friendship base has to be established first. This can take years if the new stepchildren live in distant places. It usually takes years before any trust factor can be established. It can take years before the stepchildren decide that you're even good for their mother.

The situation for a man about to form a new household with a mother and her young (under twelve) children is somewhat different. Here are suggestions, some taken from the book *Stepfathering* by Mark Bruce Rosin, some from my own experience:

- Living together before marriage creates problems. Society may be tolerant of this today, but children usually are not. Most consider it demeaning to their mother of whom they are protective. Though marriage may follow, the relationship is off to a shaky start.
- Before marriage spend time with the children, but don't overdo the gift-giving. You cannot keep it up after marriage; thus false expectations are raised.
- Go slow on showing affection to your stepchildren. Don't come on too strong. Better to let affection stem from the children and develop naturally.
- Most stepchildren will want to call you by your first name, some may call you "Dad." Let them decide, within reason.
- Establish your authority as early as possible. Children will tend to confide in their mother and go to her for permission to do this or that. The stepfather should be involved in the decision-making process as soon as possible. Get used to saying, "Your mom and I feel. . . ." Take the initiative in announcing unpopular decisions and they will gradually accept the fact that you have equal authority to impose limitations and correct their behavior.
- If you as stepfather are bringing your children to a new marriage to live together with your

new wife's children, a whole new series of problems arises: (a) the fair division of space in the home, (b) fairness in rules for bedtime, watching television, allowances, chores, use of household equipment and cars, etc., etc.

- A point to consider—you cannot have a good relationship with your new spouse without working out satisfactory relationships with her children.
- Accept the fact that your stepchildren's first loyalty will probably be, and should be, to their real father, regardless of whether he is dead or alive. This could last for many years. Do not be upset by unfair comparisons.
- Humor resolves many conflicts.
- Learn to keep a certain detachment from the emotional upsets that will doubtless occur early in the new marriage, and perhaps continue for years. Your emotional stability will become the stabilizing factor in the home.
- The best way to establish peace and order in the home is to have God at the center. Unless stepfather and mother demonstrate their commitment to the Lord, it won't take with the children. This means: (a) prayers with small children before they go to bed, (b) grace at meals, (c) an established time for family prayer and Bible reading, (d) church on Sunday.

Stepfather Strategy

When I married Catherine in 1959, her son, Peter John, was a sophomore at Yale University. He was deep into singing, dating and drinking, had no interest in the Christian faith, felt burdened by having two famous "religious" parents. I sensed at the beginning that he wanted no fatherly advice from me. Instead, we found common ground through sports. Yet Peter had been without a father since age nine. At six feet four he towered over all of us in his new family. In the ten years of his mother's widowhood, he had encountered very few strong male role models. Catherine and I agreed—he needed a spiritual encounter with a big man—big in heart and big in body.

During Catherine's and my prayers for Peter one morning early in 1961, the Lord dropped an idea into my mind: *Persuade Peter to attend the Fellowship of Christian Athletes Conference this summer.*

This sparked me. I had been involved with FCA from its inception; Catherine and I had planned to attend the August conference in Estes Park, Colorado.

The next time Peter came to our Chappaqua, New York, home for the weekend—he was now a senior—I picked what I felt was the right moment.

"Peter, how would you like to hit against Carl Erskine?" Carl had been an All-Star pitcher for the Brooklyn Dodgers.

He studied me for a moment. "Where?"

"At a summer conference at Estes Park, Colorado."

"This summer I'll be going to South America with the Yale Glee Club."

"The FCA Conference is in early August after you get back from the tour. Carl Erskine is just one of the athletes attending. Donn Moomaw will be there, too." And I named other sports figures he knew.

"I'll think about it," Peter said carefully.

Later that weekend he approached me. "This conference is religious, isn't it?" he asked.

"There will be some Christian teaching. There will also be a lot of sports activities."

"If I go, I'll skip the teaching sessions," Peter warned.

My strategy worked. I played on his deep interest in athletics and sports personalities, didn't push him too hard.

When Peter agreed to go to the conference, I made arrangements for him to have as his huddle leader Donn Moomaw, All-American linebacker from UCLA. Donn was that taller (six feet six), big-hearted man who confronted Peter about the heritage he was fleeing from, convicted him about the "pseudo-sophisticated phony" he had become, and challenged him to take a leap of faith. Peter did. A month later he was enrolled at Princeton Theological Seminary to "carry on my father's work," as he put it.

This was my first experience as stepfather to an older boy. I had no guidelines from more experienced men. Although numerous books have been written on fatherhood, I don't think there are any guidelines for being the stepfather of an adult son or daughter. Here is what I was learning.

- Be a friend first.
- Find some common ground for dialogue.
- Don't offer counsel unless he/she asks for it.
- Be careful about showing too much open affection toward his/her mother. It could bring on resentment.

- Concentrate on showing respect for your new wife. This helps increase the adult child's respect for her.
- Be aware of the pain and loss a mother and her children are working through following the divorce from or death of their previous husband and father. Be sensitive to the expressed and unexpressed feelings for him.
- Accept the fact that it may take years for you to be regarded as either a new father or friend by your wife's adult child. It might never happen. The key to bringing it off is the kind of marriage you and their mother have. If God is at the center of your marriage the adult children will usually respect it, whether they are religious or not.
- Be patient.

The experience with Peter taught me a few surprising truths. We can often help our stepchildren more by remaining in the background. For example, I didn't tell Peter I had worked it out for Donn Moomaw to be his huddle leader. If I had he could well have been suspicious and resistant.

Better to let someone else get the credit for positive results. By keeping a low profile and depending heavily on prayer, the stepfather will usually be more effective than if he tries to take charge.

Prayer Warrior Stepfather

Back in 1968 Peter had a crisis as pastor of his church in East Dennis, Massachusetts. There was a split in the congregation between those who wanted to follow Peter's leading toward a deeper walk with the Lord and those who resisted change. A meeting was called to vote on whether to retain or dismiss Peter as pastor. Catherine and I flew to Hyannis to lend him support. Since only members were allowed at the meeting, Catherine stayed home to be with their infant daughter, Mary Elizabeth, so that Edith could go and be with her husband. Was there anything I could do as stepfather?

Our good friend John Sherrill had flown up from New York to add his support. John and I decided it was important for us to hear what went on at the meeting if we were to pray effectively. But how?

It was a moonless, warm August night as we walked from the manse to the church. The frontal approach came first. We joined the line entering the church basement, and soon discovered that they were checking each person's name with a membership roster. We were outsiders. Setback number one.

Next we circled the church. Someone was guarding each door. Setback number two.

A waiting game seemed the next best strategy. We pulled back into the shadows and watched.

A careful checking of each name delayed the start of the meeting. Finally all members were inside, the basement door was closed, leaving a cluster of disgruntled nonmembers outside. One by one they drifted away. Only then did the people guarding the other doors disappear inside to participate in the meeting.

John and I stealthily approached the side entrance to the church. The door was unlocked. Quietly we opened it and eased into an inky blackness.

Crack!

I moaned softly, rubbing my leg that had knocked over a chair.

Bam!

John muttered some quiet words as he extricated himself from a coat rack.

We held our breath. Would someone appear to check out these noises? As we waited our eyes grew accustomed to the darkness. Nobody appeared.

"Over there!" John whispered.

He pointed to a staircase that led down to the basement. Probably the back entrance. Step by step we descended until we could clearly hear the voices inside through the closed door.

"Let's sit here," I suggested as we reached the bottom step. Someone was speaking for Peter.

At this point we began our silent prayers for Peter.

When someone spoke against Peter, as intercessors John and I waged spiritual warfare against the stronghold of humanism that had held the church in bondage for many years. We sat on the steps and listened and prayed throughout the entire meeting.

Finally the vote. Peter had won by the narrowest of margins! Could our prayers have made the difference?

When Your Wife Is the Stepparent

Being a stepfather to adult children brings on one set of experiences. Being the father of young children when your new wife and stepmother enters the scene creates another. Catherine, by her own admission, had been too permissive with Peter as he grew up—and I had been that way

145

with my Linda, Chet and Jeff. So I was surprised at how tough Catherine was on my three after we were married.

It wasn't the firmness of her discipline that bothered me as much as her attitude toward them.

"Why can't you be more loving to them?" I would ask.

"I can't give what I don't feel," she would reply.

One of Catherine's great attributes was her ruthless honesty, especially about her own shortcomings. But I didn't appreciate this quality as I watched my children struggle to adjust to her as their new mother . . . in a new house . . . in a different community. Our early morning prayer time was the glue that kept everything together.

Though Catherine at the beginning of our marriage could not provide the love my young children needed (this came later), she did structure our home with meals at regular times, firm hours for bedtime, when television could be watched, etc.

As I look back today on those first years of Catherine and my marriage, *I'm grateful that she was this tough.* Filled with guilt over my divorce, unaware that the years I tried to cover up my first wife's drinking had turned me into too much of a peacemaker (meaning peace at any price), I tended to give in too quickly to my children's desires and pleadings.

So the new stepmother can enter this new marriage with enough objectivity to see what the single parent cannot see—a home where the young children are in charge. Catherine saw this where I didn't. One reason she and Linda clashed from the beginning was that Linda at ten had been the real caretaker of our home amid the constant in-and-out flow of housekeepers. Catherine's arrival as stepmother meant Linda's overthrow as surrogate wife and mother—a role no child should be allowed or required to play.

An Objective Role

The single parent with young or older children just does not have the objectivity to see his/her permissiveness. Thus the new stepparent has an extremely important role to play at the beginning of the marriage, by: (a) giving balance to the home, (b) being firm where the single parent is weak, (c) teaching children discipline.

What I learned as a stepfather to Peter and watching Catherine as a stepmother to my children has prepared me for my stepparent role with Sandy's three adult children. I know I have to seek friendship first, be patient, but try to give them what Sandy cannot—a strong father role model.

The television series "Major Dad" presents in dramatic form classic confrontations faced by a stepfather who marries a woman with three daughters ranging in age from five to mid-teens. The major is conservative, disciplined, opinionated and a take-charge person. The wife is liberal, permissive, disorganized and challenging of his authority.

Opposites may attract, but when they marry each other explosions occur regularly. Viewers can learn from the major some things a new stepfather should *not* do with his new family:

- Use intimidation (it backfires)
- Make changes quickly (they create confusion, even chaos)
- Be rigid in his viewpoints (this just hardens those young people he is trying to win)

147

Today with second and third marriages (sometimes even more) for both fathers and mothers, children are understandably confused about the meaning of "family"—their place in it, their parents' place. The stepfather has to weave his way carefully through this minefield. If he does, he will grow in strength and wisdom and patience and faith:

> Let patience have its perfect work, that you may be perfect and complete, lacking nothing.
>
> James 1:4, NKJ

Questions for Reflection

1) When you are in love with a woman who has two children, eight and ten, and she wants a live-in relationship before marriage, how do you handle this?
2) What do you see as the main difference between being a stepparent to older children as over against younger children? The similarities?
3) As a stepfather how would you relate to your new stepchildren's real father if he is still alive? If he is dead?
4) What do you do as a stepfather if your young stepchildren are disrespectful to their mother? If they are disobedient?
5) How as stepfather do you handle other stepchildren when they are abusive to their mother, your new wife?

8
Worker

God . . . will not forget your work and the love you have shown him as you have helped his people and continue to help them.

Hebrews 6:10, NIV

I was in the second grade when I had this sudden urge to build a clubhouse. I knew of other kids who had club-houses but theirs were built by parents. I wanted to build one by myself, or with a couple of my buddies.

Where to build it? In the vacant tree-filled lot across from our apartment house off Watts Street in Durham, North Carolina.

Building supplies? In the basement was a pile of lumber from packing crates placed there after our recent move to Durham, from Ben Avon, Pennsylvania. Dad agreed to let me use this lumber, bought me a hammer, a saw and a box of nails.

How to begin? There was no book of instructions. I had to figure it out myself. First I chose a starting spot. Then nailed two boards together horizontally, at right angles, nailed another board to them in a vertical position. I did the same thing at the other three corners, joined the four corners together, made space for a door and I was on my way. My buddies helped me, but I was the chief builder.

Meanwhile our family was moving a lot. Through junior high school I built a total of eight clubhouses in seven different locations, including one at the summer residence of my grandparents.

When my mother moved from her New York apartment after my father's death, a yellowed sheet of paper surfaced from a trunk of her mementos. Just as I had typed them back in 1930 here are the minutes of our Newton, Massachusetts, seventh grade clubhouse:

Meetings, Laws and Other Things

The president called the meeting to order. He then called for the treasurer report it was excepted. Officers were elected. A poem was then said. Afterward games were played. The refreshments were then served which was pop corn. Then the meeting was ajurned.

Officers and important members

President—Leonard LeSourd
Treasurer—Charlie Featherstone
Secretary—John Ryan
Head carpenter—Stuart Rand

2nd Meeting

On a misty day in December the president called the meeting to order. Then he called for the tresurers report it was excepted. Laws were passed. Games were played. Then by candle light we sang songs. Afterward refreshments were served.

Laws

1.—No swearing
2.—No spitting
3.—No loafing
4.—Pay dues fairly and squarly unless folks hard up
5.—Not more than one guy on roof at one time
6.—Keep feet off table
7.—Put only printed bullentons on bullenton board
8.—Obey your superior officers

As I look back over those years I see the emergence of a talent God had given me—that of a builder. Not a builder of buildings but of organizations. My parents provided encouragement and certain supplies, but did not try to supervise and structure what we boys did.

Later as a parent I made the mistake of superimposing my childhood experiences on my children. I decided they should have a clubhouse as I had had. I then proceeded to build it for them. They seldom used it. It was Dad's, not theirs. Unless the clubhouse idea comes from deep inside a child, he or she will seldom have the drive and enthusiasm to carry it forward.

Parents who structure too many of their children's activities often stifle their creativity.

Because I had taught myself to nail boards together and saw them to the right length, my parents thought I would develop a special skill handling tools. Wrong. My carpentry skills have not advanced one whit from my junior high days.

I was drawn to team sports, was elected captain of both my junior high and high school basketball teams. In college I became editor of the yearbook, gathered together a staff to put it out. All this time I was fulfilling the Scripture: "God has given each of you some special abilities; be sure to use them to help each other" (1 Peter 4:10).

In team sports we learned to work together, *to help each other*, but at the time I was unaware of the spiritual ramifications of this talent I had been given by God. During the war I considered staying in the service as a pilot, but didn't. This wasn't my area of giftedness. Somehow on the inside I knew this.

Man and His Work

The point is this: When God creates each one of us, He implants within us as tiny embryos one or more special abilities. Some people come by their gifts naturally as I did. You can always tell when people are exercising their gifts. There is a special light in their eyes, a comfortable look on their faces.

Watch an auto mechanic attack a sick car. He listens carefully to the wheeze of the engine, cuts the switch and begins to unscrew its parts. Carefully he inspects each one. His eyes light up. He has found the trouble: a worn-out connecting rod. A replacement part is found, the parts reassembled. Then the moment of triumph. The engine is turned on. It purrs smoothly. With a satisfied smile and a glint in his eyes, he says, "It's fixed."

What did the mechanic need to fix this car? Training. Good eyesight. Strong hands. A clear mind. All these are important, but the crucial element is the special mechanical gift he was given by God.

A recent *USA Today* survey came up with some significant findings about the working man. While men as a whole have become more and more uncertain about their relationship to women, in one area they have changed little. They define their masculinity by their ability to make a living. The survey revealed that 54 percent of men ranked work as number one at what they do best. Being a father was second at 47 percent. Being a husband was third at 39 percent.

Counselors report that men ailing emotionally often will not seek therapy until their jobs are in jeopardy.

When men work at jobs they don't like, it can have more of a negative effect on their lives than a serious illness.

Why do men derive such a great sense of self-worth from their jobs? Because jobs, no matter what they are, help men define themselves and make them feel a part of something.

The survey also put this question to the worker:

If you won a million-plus in a lottery, would you tell your boss off, kick the Xerox machine and thumb your nose at the creep in accounting who keeps sending back your expense accounts?

Here's a report on 1,200 individuals who have won a million or more in the lottery:

- Four out of ten kept right on working the same jobs they had when they won the big bucks.
- Only sixteen percent retired.
- Eight out of ten said they were basically satisfied with their jobs.

What does all this add up to for a man?

His self-esteem depends largely on how good he is at his job.

It is crucial, therefore, that he finds the work that is *his*, so ordained by his Creator.

How to Find Your Gift

When Chet was graduated from college, he wasn't at all sure what he was supposed to do with his life. He was good at sports, especially tennis. He had majored in English literature, but didn't feel as if he should become a professional writer. So for the first year out of school he took a job as a tennis pro.

One summer day when the family was together at Evergreen Farm, the time seemed right for a session with Chet to "find where God wants you."

"Are you willing to do what God wants you to do?" was the first question I asked him.

"Yes."

"Are you willing to go anywhere in this world where He might want you to go?"

There was a slight pause. "Yes." Then Chet reminded me of the time at age fourteen he had attended a Fellowship of Christian Athletes conference at Black Mountain, North Carolina. The last night he had awakened to see the image of Jesus on the closed door of his room and heard the words, *You are to be one of My missionaries.* When Chet reported this vision to us, we had agreed as a family that, yes, it might mean some kind of foreign missionary service for Chet. But it could also mean that he was to be one of Christ's missionaries at whatever job he held, even as a tennis instructor.

After a time of silence while we sought direction from

God, I was led to ask this question: "In the depths of your heart, what activity do you most enjoy doing?"

Almost without thinking, Chet replied, "Work with kids."

"In what way?"

"I worked as a counselor with kids the last two summers while at college. I loved it. But it was only a summer job."

All of us sparked to this. "Chet, do you see the pattern here?" Linda spoke. "You like working with kids. You enjoy teaching tennis. You enjoy English literature. You had a great experience as a student at McCallie Boys School and won a lot of awards there." She paused. "Well . . . ?"

Chet's face was alive. "Several weeks ago I had a letter from the admissions director at McCallie asking me if I'd be interested in becoming his assistant. I wasn't. But a job as a McCallie English teacher would interest me."

"Then write the headmaster and see if such a position is available," I suggested.

Chet did. A position opened up within a matter of months for Chet to become tennis coach and an English teacher at this Chattanooga boys' school.

A great answer to prayer. We were able to help Chet find his gift and exercise it, which he has done happily now for ten years. He loves to teach kids, to watch them learn and grow, to see God-given gifts in them realized.

For a man, finding that special job that has his name on it in holy script is second only to choosing the right wife. Some men unfortunately will put finding the right work ahead of finding the right wife.

What so many men fail to realize is that God has a plan for every life He creates. He forms each life in the mother's womb with unique traits. It's mind-blowing to consider what enormous creativity God has in making every life different from the billions of other lives He has crafted. And He has His ways of steering us to the work He created us to do.

The *USA Today* survey indicates that a surprising percentage of men have found fulfillment in their jobs. I grieve for those who have not found their niche in the working world. It is there somewhere. When a man comes to a certain crossroads, a choice has to be made between one of two paths to follow:

Is he in this job for what he can get out of it?

Or what he can give to it?

The decision he makes over these two choices will dramatically determine the kind of life he leads, how his family turns out and perhaps even his health and longevity.

At the Crossroads

I remember vividly, almost as if it were yesterday, when I came to this crossroads in my late twenties. It happened in the spring of 1947. The war was over. I had written a book, *Skybent*, while in the Air Corps, so I knew writing was one possible field for me. I also had experience getting people to work together.

In 1946 I had been hired as a reporter by a small new publication called *Guideposts*. The salary was small, but I didn't feel I wanted to stay long in religious publishing anyhow. My goal was to become an editor at *Reader's Digest* or at a sports magazine.

Early on an assignment came to interview Louis Bromfield, a famous author of that day, at his farm near Mansfield, Ohio.

Malabar Farm was Bromfield's home and the title of one of his books. When I arrived by taxi at the entrance to his farm, I was met by five boxer dogs and a cocker spaniel. Bromfield, a browned, hard-muscled man stripped to his waist, appeared around the side of the farmhouse. After I introduced myself, he asked, "Would you like to join me while I plow a field? It will give us a chance to talk." I certainly would.

Looey, as everyone called him, led me to his study and tossed me some old clothes. Soon I was perched precariously on the hood of his tractor. As he plowed his field, we talked about *Guideposts*, an article he might do for us and the life of an author.

When Bromfield's article arrived a few weeks later, in his letter was a startling offer. Would I like the job of being his manager? To find out more about it, he invited me to meet him in Washington, D.C.

When I joined Bromfield in his suite at the Shoreham Hotel several days later, it didn't take me long to figure out his lifestyle. In addition to working on his farm, he enjoyed food, drink, hobnobbing with the famous and infamous. That night we went to a Pearl Mesta party, which included Clark Clifford, Margaret Truman and other notables. The next morning he made me a salary offer that was three times what I was making at *Guideposts*, plus other perks.

"You seem to take to this kind of life," Looey smiled as his spread-out hands included the whole Washington scene.

"I lived it a lot during the war."

"It's not very pious."

"I've never been a candidate for holy orders."

"Why did you take the *Guideposts* job?"

"It seemed different somehow from the kind of religion I knew as a boy."

"How so?"

"Down-to-earth. People-centered. You should know about that because you're both."

Bromfield studied me, eyes nearly closed.

"Len, you ought to face up to it. There's no future in religious journalism. Leave it to the women and old men. The strong are needed elsewhere. You're young with talent and poise. A few years with me and you'll have the contacts and the know-how to make it anywhere. Show business . . . movies . . . *Time* . . . *Life* . . . you could name it."

On the train back to New York, I mulled over the proposal. I was single, needed the kind of writing instruction Bromfield offered me and could use the extra income. Furthermore, *Guideposts* was new and shaky. If it folded, where would I be? The facts seemed to be stacked heavily toward taking this new offer.

Yet the months that I had spent writing inspirational stories for *Guideposts* had planted seeds inside me; the deadness of my spirit was beginning to lift. Meeting people who had strong beliefs stirred up hidden yearnings, a desire for something more than what I had had the past six years.

As I struggled with the decision for weeks, I focused in on one basic issue—as a man, where did I belong? What was the right job for me?

In my letter to Louis Bromfield declining his offer, I

challenged his point that religion was not the field for real men. "I've interviewed some rugged males who have not only become successful through their faith in God, they also are discovering their real identity as men. I see a future for me in this kind of inspirational journalism."

I don't believe I would have gone through such a self-examination if I hadn't taken the *Guideposts* job. For at this struggling small publication I was already giving more than I received—and being enriched in the process. Funds were so short that when the mail arrived each day, the few of us in the office would open letters together to see if enough subscription and contribution money had come to pay our salaries. Somehow there always was enough—and this was faith-building.

The Lord of the Work

Soon after my decision to stay at *Guideposts* came the decision to accept Jesus Christ as Lord of my life. I now had a different measuring rod for everything I did at work, at home or at play.

I had done "the work of the Lord" at *Guideposts* for several years, aware that being involved with this worthwhile venture would somehow rub off on me, but thinking of it mostly as a steppingstone to a bigger job in a bigger publication. A whole new concept began forming inside me about the "how of my work" as I learned to put the Lord first in my life.

And so almost before I knew what was happening I had a new credo: *Depend on the Lord of the work, not the work of the Lord.*

For example, I had been handicapped at work in one

159

important area—a fear of public speaking. In one-on-one situations or with a few friends, no problem, but before even a small audience my brain would seem to freeze as I stood before them and I would struggle red-faced to get out a few sentences. Through artful ducking and excuse-making I had gotten by with only a few embarrassing situations.

A *Guideposts* interview gave me the handle to free myself of this handicap. It was with Roland Hayes, the great black baritone.

Before each concert, Roland Hayes would stand quietly in front of his audience, hands clasped together, eyes closed, silently praying: *Lord, You are my strength; You are my voice. Help me get Roland Hayes out of the way so that You can sing through me, so that Your music and words can touch the hearts of these people.*

"If I forget to say this prayer," Mr. Hayes told me, "then I tend to think of myself and how I'm doing. As a result, the concerts just don't seem to have the same power and impact. What God does through me is so much greater than what I can do on my own."

He told the story of the toughest audience he ever faced. It was in Germany before World War II at a time when racial hostility was rampant there. When he appeared on the stage, some of the people started to boo and hiss because he was black.

Roland Hayes never faltered. He closed his eyes, folded his hands and silently prayed: *Lord, You sing through me and melt this hatred.*

Minutes went by while the hissing continued. The quiet figure on the stage never moved. Finally, the huge hall was quiet. Then he began to sing very softly. For an hour and a half he sang while the spectators sat there as if transfixed. At the end the audience rose as a body and gave him a tremendous ovation.

"The glory goes to God," Mr. Hayes told me. "There's nothing He can't do through us if we would only get ourselves out of the way."

It made a strong story when I prepared it for *Guideposts*. Most important for me was the personal application. "Self-centeredness is the problem when one has stage fright," the singer had stated.

That was my problem, all right—self-centeredness. The solution—depend on the Lord of the work and get self out of the way. Armed with this approach I decided to accept every speaking opportunity that arose. Within a year this fear had been conquered.

We ran a story by an Atlanta housewife who told how putting a picture of Jesus Christ on her living room wall had helped bring about a change in the atmosphere of her home. The result was fewer family upsets, a higher level of conversation, more love.

"If it can happen in a home, why not in the office?" I asked myself. I mounted on my office wall a picture of Jesus in His robes sitting by the desk of a contemporary businessman. Result: a change in atmosphere, less tension in the way I did things. I became more aware of my language, found myself checked regularly in all manner of decisions by His presence.

An article on "prayer without ceasing" started my having running conversations with the Lord as I walked to work. Facing a difficult interview I found myself saying, "How do I handle this person, Lord? They say he has a good story, but is hard to talk to." Before an important phone call, I would stop and say, "Lord, will You put just the right words in my mouth?"

The Lord of my work gave me a check on my tendency to crowd my schedule too full, which often made me late for appointments. *You are robbing that person of his time,* the inner voice spoke. *You cheated him out of twenty minutes.* When I saw it from this point of view, I also realized I did it because an overly full schedule made me feel important. Self-centeredness again. From then on I lightened my schedule and put a high priority on being on time.

So what slowly developed was a new picture of my role as a worker. The work becomes bigger than the office . . . or the factory . . . or the brickyard . . . or the school . . . and is not done so much for the boss, or for profit, or for recognition—it is performed for the Lord. He is the Lord of the work. Done this way there is much less strain, for He helps carry the load.

The Lord of the work also shows you how to deal with setbacks. When it became obvious that *Guideposts* had the potential to be a major magazine, Grace Perkins Oursler was hired as executive editor. I would be the associate editor under her. Now I had a woman boss. For many years Grace had been a prominent writer herself and a passionate advocate of Christian causes. The thought of having to bring my work to her for acceptance or rejection was a blow.

In time, because of her flair, her warmth, her generosity, I came to love Grace as a person. Yet it still was hard for me to accept her authority. In the Air Corps the system made it easy: I accepted my rank and was obedient to those higher up whether they warranted it or not. It was not up to me, a junior officer, to judge the competence of senior officers. When hired by Dr. Peale, he was my boss. No problem here for me. But with Grace it was soon obvious that her experience was in writing, not editing. Since she knew so little about the various stages of putting out a magazine, I had to teach her, yet obey her.

Once again I turned to the Lord of my work. He referred me to *The Practice of the Presence of God* by Brother Lawrence, a Carmelite lay brother, who for long stretches of time did menial tasks in the kitchen of a monastery. Every day he dedicated his very ordinary, often dirty work to the Lord. Once this was done, he carried out his tasks with such joy and overflowing love that the work itself became a blessing to everyone about him.

One day while chafing over my situation with Grace, I began thinking about Brother Lawrence's amazing capacity to find God in every little facet of his daily life. The head brother of the monastery might say that Brother Lawrence was working for them. But not Lawrence. He would be working for the Lord because he considered himself the Lord's person in that particular job.

This thought changed my attitude. I worked under Grace, but not for her. She and I both worked under Dr. Peale, but not for him. Since I was the Lord's person at *Guideposts*, I worked for Him.

In 1953 Grace Oursler passed away. I was soon given the title of executive editor. The full responsibility of the *Guideposts* editorial process was now mine.

My days as a worker were not over. They had simply changed. Meanwhile, what had I learned from my work experience?

God had given me certain gifts. I was learning to use them.

163

Work done for personal gain dulls my spirit; work that produces something beyond myself excites me.

Inviting God into my work opens the door for new creativity.

Being in the right job, doing the kind of work where I give more than I receive brings a whole new light onto my strength as a man.

Questions for Reflection

1) Do you feel you have discovered your special God-given gift or gifts? If not, why not?
2) How can you tell whether a gift or talent you have is of God? Of man?
3) Can you give an example of a God-given talent being misused?
4) Where is work on your priority list? If it's number one, should you rethink your priorities?
5) How do you see God relating to your job?

9
Boss

"[Lord], say the word, and my servant will be healed. For I also am a man placed under authority, having soldiers under me. And I say to one, 'Go,' and he goes . . . and to my servant, 'Do this,' and he does it."

Luke 7:7–8, NKJ

By invitation from Malcolm Forbes, multimillionaire head of the Forbes Publishing Company, some 800 people attended his widely publicized seventieth birthday party in Morocco in August 1989—all expenses paid. The Concorde and another jet were rented to transport the guests to the party. Forbes spent two million dollars on this bash.

Reaction by Americans was mixed, some openly admiring, others sharply critical at what they felt was an offensive display of wealth. "Money and flamboyant consumption are what America stands for," it seemed to say to the world.

It certainly was what Forbes stood for. When he died in February 1990 the epitaph he asked for his tombstone read: "While alive he lived." He lived so flamboyantly he became a symbol of the excesses of the 1980s; he rode motorcycles, piloted hot-air balloons, owned a chateau in France, a palace in Tangier and a South Sea island. A more definitive epitaph might be the placard he kept on his desk: "He who dies with the most toys wins."

During the greedy 1980s, becoming a millionaire no longer excited aggressive, money-hungry people as it once did. In some parts of the country you could spend a million dollars just buying a home. Billionaire became the new buzz word. At latest count there were 144 known billionaires in the world.

The result of this obsession to make money: stock market scandals, illegal get-rich business schemes, Congress forcing its leaders to resign because of ethics violations, athletic programs in major colleges devastated by greed.

There's something sad, almost pathetic about the super rich. They are indeed like little boys gathering toys about them: an airline here, a candy company there, here a baseball team, there a pants factory, the inevitable yacht, of course, and homes or condominiums scattered about the world. They put on lavish parties, cozy up to film celebrities and may even have a pet charity.

Strong men? Hardly. Many have demonstrated a talent to make money by destroying smaller companies and trampling on people in the process. Not many have captured the vision of how to use their money to make a better world.

The Love of Money

Many years ago a wealthy young man was excited by the words of a new Teacher in his area. He felt a sudden, inner urge to be a part of this work. The Teacher saw the rich man's problem the minute they began to talk.

"Sell all you have and give the money to the poor—it

will become treasure for you in heaven—and come follow Me," Jesus told him (see Luke 18:18–24).

The wealthy man saw the two choices before him and hesitated. His spirit said, "Do it," but his bondage to his assets was too strong. He shook his head and turned sadly away from the new life offered him, never to be heard from in the Bible again.

The love of money has been a trap for men down through the centuries, eroding their creativity, destroying their value systems. A few escape and learn that their financial abilities and leadership can be used by God to benefit people in extraordinary ways.

Millard Fuller, for example. As a boy Millard had a knack for making money. Through livestock trading in his teens he paid his way through college. At law school he and a partner sold desk blotters, campus directories and holly wreaths, investing their profits in real estate.

After graduation, Fuller launched a mail-order business, determined to be a millionaire by age thirty. He made it with a year to spare. Yet two things were wrong.

One, he had trouble breathing at times as if a heavy weight were pressing on his chest.

Two, his wife, Linda, was unhappy. "I feel as if I don't have a husband," she told him one day. "You're always working. I don't think we have a future together." She left Millard to go to New York City and think things over.

Crisis time. Millard had his bank statement showing his monetary worth of a million dollars, but what did it mean if he lost the woman he loved? Time alone helped him see how wrong his priorities had been. Work had been first, family second. God hardly appeared in the picture at all. For the first time he sought God's direction for his life.

Millard then sought out Linda and dropped his bomb-shell: "I've decided to give all my money away and let God run my life. Let's go home and start all over again."

Linda was stunned. She laughed. She cried. They went home and Millard did exactly what he said he was going to do. He sold his part of the business and distributed the proceeds to churches and charities.

His marriage was restored, the heavy weight lifted from his chest, and they began to look for a work that would honor the Lord and bless people.

Habitat for Humanity was the result. It began when Fuller saw a need for better housing in the poor section of Americus, Georgia. A corporation was set up, donations sought. The capital would go for land and building mate-rials. The corporation would construct simple, decent houses and sell them at cost.

A key part of the plan—the homebuyers were encour-aged to put many hours of work into the construction of their own homes. Others also volunteered their time and skills. In fact, they would come from miles away to work.

After we told Millard Fuller's story in *Guideposts* several years ago, I went down to Americus to learn more about Habitat. I found Millard on the roof of a house pounding nails into some roof sheathing. Since local papers had pub-licized the project, passersby were stopping to gawk.

"Who's paying all these people to do this work?" one asked.

"Nobody," Millard replied.

The man shook his head. "Folks don't do this sort of work for nothing."

Millard grinned at him and then waved his arm indicat-ing other workers in houses being built nearby. "None of them is being paid. In fact, they paid to come to work."

The onlooker was impressed. "That's real religion."

Since then this idea has taken hold throughout the world. Habitat for Humanity in 1981 had 15 projects in the United States, 11 overseas. By 1990 there were 460 projects in North America and 85 in 29 countries abroad. More than 2000 Habitat houses were built in 1989 with volunteer workers including former President Jimmy Carter and his wife, Rosalynn.

Shortage of Leaders

Though we have a plethora of men obsessed with earning big bucks today throughout the world, we have an alarming shortage of real leaders. What is the answer? Can we learn from the past?

Ever since He created the world, God has had a problem with the men He tapped to be leaders. Adam disobeyed God's warning not to eat the fruit of the tree of life. Cain blew it when he murdered his brother. Noah did great with the ark, but slipped when he gave in to the lure of his wine.

God singled out Abraham and said to him: "Leave your own country behind you, and your own people, and go to the land I will guide you to. If you do, I will cause you to become the father of a great nation. I will bless you and you will be a blessing to many others" (see Genesis 12:1–3).

What was God looking for in the men He chose for leadership? Men who would listen to His Word—and then obey it. Adam didn't do it. Noah did. Abraham did.

I have learned a lot from the Bible about leadership. I

mentioned earlier that while at *Guideposts* I began meeting weekly with a group of my church friends.

One night in an East Side apartment, one of our group talked about leadership. "Moses is considered to be one of the giant leaders of all time," he began. "Well, he sure gets off to a slow start." Then he pointed out that when God tells Moses he's to lead his people out of bondage in Egypt, Moses ducks (see Exodus 3–4):

> "Who am I, that I should bring the children of Israel out of Egypt?"

This could be proper modesty, so the Lord assures Moses, "I will be with you." Then Moses says:

> "But they [the Israelites] will not believe me."

God is patient. He tells Moses that he will be given the power to perform miracles. Moses is impressed but then says:

> "I am slow of speech, and slow of tongue."

The Lord seems to be losing patience with Moses, but He continues His reassurance, saying, "I will be with your mouth and teach you what to say." Yet Moses still resists, saying:

> "Lord, I pray Thee, send someone else."

Probably fed up with Moses now, the Lord finally tells him to quit squirming and get his brother, Aaron, to help him out, which Moses does.

A young salesman began nodding his head vigorously at this. "That's just like me. I felt very inadequate when I began selling. Like Moses, I had a slow tongue. But the Lord was with me just as He was with Moses. Last year I went from eighth to third in sales in our division."

Your Ideas, Lord

One day as I was reading through a batch of manuscripts in my office, planning for the months ahead, a ray of light pierced my thinking. *Why don't you depend on Me to help you develop this magazine?*

I stopped reading to ponder this. The teaching on Moses was fresh in my thinking. I sure needed help. So I asked my two associate editors, John Sherrill and Starr West Jones, if they would be willing to stay late for a special evening session to brainstorm editorial ideas. The answer: definitely yes. An artist who was doing layouts for us— Norm Mullendore—was also invited, plus a newspaper columnist and a writer both of whom later became *Guideposts* roving editors—Sidney Fields and Glenn Kittler.

As we gathered around a small table in the office, I took a deep breath and suggested we open the discussion with prayer. "Lord," I said, "we have an opportunity to reach many people through this magazine. Please give us Your help and Your ideas."

A lively give-and-take session followed as a group of professionals used their talents to try to produce an excellent literary product. Yet something was different. For the first time we were seeking God's specific help and direction.

There had been an early dedication of *Guideposts* to God

as an organization; there had been petitions for His help during times of emergency. Now we were inviting the Lord into the editorial office to be a part of the pen-to-paper, everyday functioning of the magazine. We had also begun to pray that He would send us the people He wanted to be a part of the work. And I was on the way to discovering what every boss should know: His basic need is to *surround himself with people who have what he doesn't have.*

By 1956 we had moved the editorial office to the seventh floor of the Carnegie Building, located on United Nations Plaza. Our space was now doubled. As I opened up our editorial meeting with prayer one day, I noted that now around the table were ten people, including four new ones He had sent us: Elizabeth Sherrill, Van Varner, Arthur Gordon, Dina Donohue.

The purpose of that meeting was to come up with new features.

I read a letter from one of our subscribers:

> Most of us who read your magazine are just plain folks. We can't identify with Hollywood actors and bank presidents. Give us more of the little people.

"She's got a point here," I said. "Yet stories by well-known people are important because they draw readers into the magazine."

"How about a regular feature, which we could call 'Just Plain Folks,' " suggested Sidney Fields.

"Sounds like a soap opera."

"Wait a minute. Sidney's onto something here."

"How about calling them 'Little People'?"

"Sounds like a bunch of midgets."

"We want short features about average men and women who go about quietly doing something worthwhile for others in the community," I summarized.

"Quiet people."

"That's it!"

And so one of *Guideposts'* most successful short features was born and is still appearing in the magazine now 35 years later. This happened over and over. We asked the Lord for new ideas, went about our business and the prayer was answered almost without our being aware of it.

As a leader I was learning that the less I forced my convictions upon the editorial group, the freer they were to speak out. As a result more honest convictions were expressed instead of comments voiced to please the boss. I soon recognized that everyone on staff had a gift superior to mine: John Sherrill and his great story sense; Starr West Jones with his organizational skills; Arthur Gordon's ability to write about the common in an uncommon way; Elizabeth Sherrill's magic with words as she uncovered the "takeaway" of every article; Van Varner's compassion; Sal Lazarrotti's flair; Dina Donohue's memory.

When I married Catherine in 1959, she joined the *Guideposts* staff, blessing us with her exceptional writing talent along with her in-depth knowledge of Scripture.

For years, I have pondered the matter of my own strengths in leadership. If I succeed in subduing my ego, what will be left? Can humility be a form of self-deception? Is not the person who tries to demonstrate humility a sort of hypocrite because he feels that this is the way to impress people? What if I succeed in being humble only to have people walk all over me?

I have struggled with these questions in the process of building editorial staffs for two organizations. Two brief case histories:

A woman employee years ago was efficient but deceptive. Several times we caught her in small acts of dishonesty. We talked with her, prayed for her, but while she would admit her deception, our concern never brought about any repentance or change. For almost two years the office was in a state of unrest until we finally let her go, yet with a feeling of failure.

An assistant editor showed ability, but had strange periods of fuzzy-mindedness. I explained to him carefully why he was not doing the job before letting him go. A few years later I had a thank-you letter from him saying how being fired helped him to face up to his problem with alcohol.

I learned from those two experiences that the boss should consider two main questions when he contemplates discharging an employee: (a) What's good for the staff? (b) What's good for the erring worker? The boss is tempted to think he is somehow being "more Christian" if he is longsuffering and tolerant with an employee who is not doing the job.

Wise King Solomon said it best: "Putting confidence in an unreliable man [or employee] is like chewing with a sore tooth, or trying to run on a broken foot" (Proverbs 25:19, LB).

As the years passed, *Guideposts* became a remarkable success story, growing in circulation from a few thousand to its present circulation of four-and-a-half million subscribers.

After 28 years with *Guideposts*, I resigned in 1974 to join

John and Elizabeth Sherrill in launching a new Christian book publishing company: Chosen Books.

The Hunger for Leaders

Great male leaders are almost nonexistent today. Those who have promise go through an intense media scrutiny that probes for and usually finds weaknesses. As a result, potential leaders steer away from public service. Yet there is a hunger in people everywhere for strong men to come onto the international scene and solve our world problems. Could any man, no matter how brilliant, measure up to our ideal of great leadership?

That *Time* magazine would choose Mikhail Gorbachev, a Communist leader, as its "Man of the Decade" of the 1980s dismayed many people. Yet it made a statement about our worldwide leadership vacuum.

With the demands upon leaders perhaps three times what they were fifty years ago, required reading for every boss could well be these verses from the book of Proverbs:

Proud men end in shame, but the meek become wise.

Pride leads to arguments; be humble, take advice and become wise.

Winking at sin leads to sorrow; bold reproof leads to peace.

Anyone willing to be corrected is on the pathway to life. Anyone refusing has lost his chance.

Abraham Lincoln showed his leadership greatness in the humble way he dealt with his associates. Once during

175

the Civil War he sat in the office of his top general for half an hour, waiting to confer with him. When asked why the President of the United States would subordinate himself to one of his generals in such a manner, the President replied simply, "He was busier than I was."

On another occasion, Lincoln accepted severe criticism and a humiliating snub from his Secretary of State, William Henry Seward. When asked what he was going to do about such insulting behavior, Lincoln replied, "Nothing. Mr. Seward's performance as Secretary is all that matters right now."

This kind of behavior from a boss may not fit the image many have of the dynamic leader, but you sense that Lincoln read the book of Proverbs. And the Gospels. He trusted God and cared for his people. The same is true of the centurion who came to Jesus and said, "Lord, my servant is lying at home paralyzed, dreadfully tormented."

Jesus said to him, "I will come and heal him."

The centurion answered, "Lord, I am not worthy that You should come under my roof. Speak the word and he will be healed. For I am also a man under authority, having soldiers under me. And I say to this one, 'Go,' and he goes and to my servant, 'Do this,' and he does it."

Jesus marveled at the centurion's humility and faith and caring leadership and He healed the servant. (See Matthew 8:5–13.)

Frank Rogers is one executive who has learned to combine a caring heart for people with tough-mindedness. As head of a small business, Frank started out feeling that he had to be a dominating, demanding leader. As a result, his employees worked under tension, creativity was suppressed and the business floundered.

After several visits to our Bible study group Frank decided to make some changes at his business. He told his employees one day: "God is now running this company." He instituted a tithing program for the firm, and every Monday morning gathered his people together to pray for company and individual concerns.

It was as if an enormous shot of adrenalin had been pumped into the company. Creativity increased sharply. Soon a family-like atmosphere pervaded the place.

When the company moved into larger new quarters a few years later, the harmony of relationships was threatened. Some of the offices were smaller than expected; the modern design did not appeal to everyone. Frank was bothered by what he felt was a lack of appreciation on the part of his people.

One Saturday afternoon he entered the new quarters to work on a report. The plant was quiet and deserted as he walked through the freshly painted corridors to his office. For a moment, Frank sat at his desk, ruminating over the recent move. It obviously had not been handled as well as it should. What had gone wrong?

The answer came: "We have lost the intimacy we had in the old place." Yet growth and change, he reasoned, were a part of life; the move had been necessary. Then, as Frank expressed it to us later, it was as if a special revelation was given him of the problems, confusions and needs of his employees. Suddenly, a great love for each one of the forty-plus people in his company swept over him.

He got up and walked into the office of Ben, his plant manager. Because of Frank's open-door policy as boss, none of his employees felt moved to lock their offices. He sat in Ben's chair and studied the family picture on the desk. Ben's wife, Ann, had been in poor health for six months now. The two daughters were in college, a real drain on their finances. No wonder Ben was edgy and humorless.

"Lord, as I sit in Ben's chair, help me to understand him better, to feel a bit as he feels, to see the plant through his eyes."

Then Frank thought of the long hours Ben worked and the many times he had asked for an assistant. Frank had resisted this as an unnecessary expense. Now, suddenly, he saw it differently. Ben needed help and he should be training a younger man.

Next Frank sat at the desk of Janet, his long-time secretary. Janet was middle-aged, divorced and lived alone. The move of her office had been hard on Janet because she was resistant to change. As Frank prayed for her, he suddenly understood her occasional waspishness. Loneliness erodes one's good nature; it can diminish faith. Janet needed more change, not less. Perhaps he could give her some special travel assignments.

For three hours Frank went from desk to desk, sitting in the chair of each employee, in a sense stepping into their shoes for a moment and presenting them to God as valued persons, both to him as an employer and to God as their Father. It was a moving and emotional experience, bringing tears on occasion and resulting in so many ideas that he had to write them down on paper.

"The Spirit of God poured through me that afternoon," he told me later. "I saw things about my people I hadn't understood before. I could hardly wait for Monday to come so that I could put His ideas into action."

No need to state that Frank's company continued to grow and prosper.

Eight Leadership Principles

Some of the things I have learned in 44 years of publishing:

1) Know the people under your authority. Learn something of their family lives so that you can congratulate them on an award, commiserate over an illness or a death.

2) At least once a year write a personal note of gratitude to each employee, referring to some specific aspect of work well done.

3) Do not hesitate to terminate the employment of an employee who does poor work. Often such a person is in the wrong job, or persisting in wrong behavior, and being fired will often wake the employee up.

4) A boss is first a servant. There should be no job so menial, no job so repetitive that the leader wouldn't do it or hasn't already done it himself.

5) Remember this principle: *What the boss is speaks so loud it is hard to hear what he says.* If your behavior is offensive in any way, your authority and position are weakened.

6) A workaholic boss often produces workaholic employees to the detriment of all the families involved. If you as leader have priorities in this order, (a) God, (b) family, (c) job, you

and your employees will be happier, health-
ier and more productive.

7) Create both short-term and long-term goals
for your organization and post them in a
prominent place. Example: At *Guideposts* we
posted this goal in 1950—100,000 subscribers
by 1953. We made it.

8) Pray for your people and their families daily.

Questions for Reflection

1) Do you pray for leaders? If so, how?
2) Do you see yourself as a leader or follower?
How would you like to change your situation?
3) What do you feel is the most important quality a boss should have? Why?
4) What do you feel is the main reason a man
fails at being a good boss?
5) How should one train to become a good
leader?

10
Competitor

The one thing I do . . . is to forget what is behind me and do my best to reach what is ahead. So I run straight toward the goal in order to win the prize.

Philippians 3:13–14, GNB

It was a semifinals match in a mixed-doubles tournament. My partner and I were underdogs against the top-seeded team. The match was close, one set apiece, three games each in a tough third set.

Then it happened. A high lob came to me, short. I aimed my overhead smash between our two opponents. Plunk! The ball veered to the left and hit Bertha on the shoulder. Point for us.

"Sorry!" I called out.

Bertha, the experienced woman competitor on the opposing team, had not played well. She grimaced, threw down her racquet in anger, and clutched her shoulder. An appeal for spectator sympathy? Real pain?

I apologized again, concerned that I might have hurt her. Inside, I was kicking myself. *Why do you have to get so competitive in a mixed-doubles match?*

From then on I aimed my shots away from Bertha. Instantly, my partner and I lost our touch. Then, as Bertha began playing her best tennis, we lost the match, too.

When we shook hands afterwards, I apologized again to Bertha. She would not look me in the eyes. It was all so clear now. I had been a victim of her gamesmanship.

For days afterward I was bothered by this incident and my handling of it. Not so much over my errant shot, which was unintentional and part of the game, but because I let the episode and Bertha's exploitation of it drain away my competitiveness.

Why did I let up? Was it guilt over the intensity of my play against a woman? Did I think a Christian should not care so much about winning?

As I had done many times before, I reexamined my approach to competition. "Run the race to win," goes that passage in the New Testament. Each of us is born with a competitive nature. It's there for a reason. Earliest man needed this inner drive to defend himself against predators, to find food, to protect his woman and children. He had no question about his identity. Only the fit survived.

As civilization developed, man used his competitive spirit in a number of ways: to make a better living for himself and his family, to compete in games, to fight wars. True, man's competitive nature can turn into something ugly . . . violent . . . abusive. The Romans, for example. Two thousand years ago they came to the Forum to see blood flow; man against man, man against beast. The savage nature will always be there in some men, especially when nourished by alcohol and other drugs.

In recent years we have seen the obsession to win get out of hand. It was George Allen, coach of the Washington Redskins in the 1970s, who summed it up after his team lost a championship game: "Losing is death."

I can identify with fan frenzy over a big victory. There is

an intoxication when your team wins a championship after months of struggle, even a kind of ecstasy when it happens in the bottom of the ninth or with a last-minute touchdown or a fifty-foot jump shot at the buzzer. But when I look at a scene of delirium with screaming and foot-stomping and hand-waving and rolling on the ground, I stop and say, "This is just a game. Six months from now who will care? Why don't they get this excited about something important?"

But competition is a part of life, we are told. It begins in kindergarten or before and continues throughout life—at home, at work, in play, even in church. The man who can't or won't compete is a—well, there's that word we hear so often . . .

Wimp.

Men would rather be called almost anything but that four-letter word for namby-pambyness. "A wimp is one whose spirit of competition is dead," they say.

The Other Side

Just when I felt I had the issue of competitor settled in my mind, I met Stuart at a Washington, D. C., conference. After one of the meetings we talked. Since Stuart heads up a small ministry, I asked him what a Christian's position should be on competition, knowing he would have a definite opinion.

"If a man is ruled by the spirit of competition, he is always coming against people, vying with them, trying to beat them," he stated. "This can hardly be God's nature in man, for God works *with* and *through* people, not *against* them."

"Christ came against the moneychangers and threw them out of the Temple," I pointed out.

"But Christ was coming against evil. That's different. Jesus was never competitive with people in anything He said or did."

"How about His attacks against the Pharisees?"

"Evil again."

"As a boy didn't Jesus play games with His brothers and sisters? If He didn't run and play with His peers He would have been ostracized," I suggested.

"Maybe He was ostracized. There is some indication that He was not close to His brothers and sisters."

"You are saying that in His day Jesus might have been called a wimp."

"Jesus has been called many things the past two thousand years. The term *wimp* is pretty mild in comparison," he replied. "Remember, Jesus stressed again and again that He came to serve people. And servanthood is the opposite of competition."

I enjoyed my jousts with Stuart because he aroused my competitive spirit. When I told him so he laughed.

"I'm not saying your competitive spirit is evil, or necessarily wrong, Len," he said. "I think we all get trapped into behavior that is not of God."

When Competition Begins

We ended up agreeing to disagree. But he made me think still deeper about the subject, which resulted in my going 'way back to my childhood to see how and when the seeds of competition were planted in me.

At age six I remember playing "kick the can" in the

street in front of our house. One person became "it." He stood by the can, closed his eyes and counted to ten while the other children ran to hide. When he found one, he ran to touch the can and that person was caught. But if a person in hiding beat the hunter to home base and kicked the can, everyone caught was free to hide again.

The excitement in this game for me was to free those caught. A fairly lofty purpose for a six-year-old.

Then there was that memorable childhood experience when I was in the third grade at Watts Street Elementary School in Durham, North Carolina. By now I was grabbing the sports page of the newspaper as soon as it arrived. When I learned to shoot marbles—a major pastime for kids in Durham back then—the school playground became my area of paradise.

One sport seemed out of reach for me—football. I was small for my age and the game was always played by bigger boys. Yet I always hoped to be one of those chosen to play in the pick-up tackle games that took place after school in a nearby vacant lot. I dreamed of making the spectacular play that would astonish the older boys. Day after day I stood on the sideline, yearning to play but always being overlooked because of my size. Then one day it happened.

"Hey, kid!"

Startled, I looked at the large boy headed my way. He had tousled orange hair, a torn blue sweater, filthy brown pants and a good-natured, lopsided grin. Everyone called him Crane.

"We're short a man. Wanna play?"

I fell down in my eagerness to get on the field and join Crane's team. Having never competed before, I just dashed about, bumping into players, sprawling on the soft red clay, wiping the dirt off my clothes after each play. But Crane encouraged rather than ridiculed me.

Playing guard next to the center, I was positioned where I could do the least damage. Then with Crane running the ball, we scored a touchdown. Jumping up and down with excitement, I suddenly felt as big and ferocious as a tiger.

We kicked off to the other team and I tore down the field after the burly kid who caught the ball. I had never made a tackle in my life, yet I had watched it done. You simply dove into the ball-carrier's knees.

Running with one-eyed intensity, I darted by the opposing players, who let me through probably because they didn't think I was big enough to bother with. Suddenly I was all alone facing this husky kid who was a head taller and nearly twice my weight.

I never slowed up. With head down and shoulders hunched, I tore into him. With the impact I saw every star in the heavens, but he fell down hard right on top of me. Stunned, I lay there for a moment.

"You O.K., kid?" Crane's face was blurred above me.

My forehead was smeared with red clay, there was the salt taste of blood in my mouth and my head was spinning. Yet I jumped up cockily.

"I'm O.K. Let's go."

A wide grin spread over Crane's face. "Way to go, Shorty!" He pounded me on the back. "You got it, kid."

The hurts were forgotten. The words of praise created a feeling of intoxication. My pain became a kind of ecstasy. The world stopped for a moment while I drank in the sweet words, *Way to go, Shorty.*

That one play created an image for me—and a new

name. From then on every time we met in the school hallway Crane, a sixth-grader, would single me out with, "Way to go, Shorty." I soon developed a wild aggressiveness in every sport to maintain my image.

I grew up idolizing sports figures. As a young teenager in Newton, Massachusetts, I studied the sports pages, hung on the radio broadcasts of games, went at every opportunity to see the Boston Red Sox compete at Fenway Park or the Boston Bruins play hockey at the Boston Garden. I would swing from wild jubilation to abject despair depending on how my teams performed. In the 1930s, 1940s and into the 1950s, like most sports fans I saw only the good side of our heroes. Reporters had an unwritten agreement not to reveal in their newspaper stories the heavy drinking and womanizing and other misbehavior they saw going on among sports celebrities.

Today—reality. I have to face this question: If competition is good, why is the sports scene so sick and out of control? It isn't necessary to document all the abuses, just a few. . . .

- Unruly fans who destroy property. Some European soccer games have even ended in riots.
- The greed of owners and players as they grapple for the huge profits, mostly from television.
- Strikes by players for more, always more.
- Drug and alcohol abuse by players resulting in suspension, even death.
- Breaking of rules against use of steroids (Ben Johnson, for instance), betting on games in which players or managers are involved (Pete

Rose), putting illegal substances on balls by pitchers, etc.

- The recruiting wars where college coaches and friends of the school give illegal, under-the-table payments to athletes.

The philosophy today for some modern players might be summed up by this whimsical statement by Houston Astro relief pitcher Larry Andersen: "What I want is less to do, more time to do it and to get paid more for not getting it done."

The Good News

As I think through the issue of man's competitiveness, I come back to some basics. What strength do men receive from competition? A sense of comradeship? Fair play?

There is a healthy innocence about young boys gathered together at a playground competing for a position on the local baseball team. They throw, they catch, they hit the ball, they run. Some do it better than others. Then they become a team and start playing games.

* A batter gets on first base with a hit. The coach tells the next batter, "Sacrifice." He does, tapping the ball softly to the pitcher and is thrown out at first so that the runner on first can go to second base.

Team play. You deny yourself by not doing what you would like to do—hit the ball for a home run. Instead, you bunt your teammate to second so he has a better chance to score.

Wise coaches teach players to sacrifice themselves for the good of the team. Wonderful training for the husband

and father-to-be. Team play learned as a boy can help one in every area of life. It has for me.

Too bad that the player who makes the most sacrifices for his team doesn't get the same recognition as the one who hits the most home runs. Team play should be recognized in every sport.

Misbehaving athletes receive heavy media focus, while the many high-minded competitive men who have battled the abuses, taken a stand on morality, stressed self-discipline, get little attention in the press for these qualities.

Carl Erskine, one of the Brooklyn Dodger greats, received wide media attention when he pitched two no-hitters. Few heard about the patient, loving way he handled his son Jimmy, born with Downs Syndrome. Carl and his wife, Betty, spent hours teaching, training, integrating Jimmy into the family. The end result was that their other three children not only learned a new kind of love and compassion, but had invaluable lessons in self-sacrifice and patience.

Clyde King, former pitcher, coach and manager on various major league baseball teams, found ways to turn his competitive nature into service for the Lord. As manager of the San Francisco Giants some years ago, Clyde offered to buy breakfast for anyone on his team who would join him in church. He almost won the pennant his first year as manager, but got fired the second when his star player wanted to make the rules and the owner backed him.

Firings are a part of the game he loved, Clyde told me once. They never kept him from being the man God created him to be.

Clyde moved on to a job with George Steinbrenner and

the New York Yankees. As manager Clyde soon had differences with the owner and was fired. Yet because Steinbrenner so respected Clyde's personal integrity and baseball knowledge, he made him a key person in the Yankee organization where he has been serving for eleven years.

Then there was John Wooden, legendary basketball coach of UCLA, whose teams from 1974 to 1981 captured the national championship six times.

When I interviewed Coach Wooden back in 1970, he talked nostalgically about playing basketball in grade school when players had to buy their own jerseys and shoes. "I often played with my jersey on top of my overalls," he recalled.

Once Wooden forgot to bring his jersey and shoes to school the day of a game. When he asked the coach to excuse him from a class to go home and get them, the coach refused. "No special favors, Johnny. We'll miss you today."

When Wooden's school lost the game, the coach took him aside afterward and said, "Johnny, we could have won with you in there, but winning isn't the most important thing, is it?"

Coach Wooden, whose teams featured enthusiasm, loyalty and team spirit, reminded me of Guy Baker, my coach back in the 1930s at Bigelow Junior High in Newton. Mr. Baker cared deeply about his boys and the character each was forming. Once he caught me in a lie and kept me out of a baseball game. At the time I was devastated, but the lesson in honesty has stuck with me to this day.

Competition at Home

As I have struggled with the competition issue, my friend and associate John Sherrill has stretched my thinking. John is not an athlete, but he is fiercely competitive in his own field—writing. And his chief competition has come from a surprising corner.

John and Elizabeth (Tib) married as both were starting their junior years in college. John was used to being at the top of his class. Only now there was a student who got better grades than he did.

His wife.

The competition continued when both became professional writers. Once an editor of a major magazine asked John and Tib to write a two-part article. They did. The editor accepted Tib's, returned John's. John was steamed for a while, then got back his perspective.

They tried writing under a joint byline to ease the domestic tension. That didn't work either.

Competition, they decided, was an important component of living beings. It compels one tree to crowd out another on the forest floor. It draws a rutting ram to crash into a competing male with a shock report that can be heard for miles. The stronger tree gets the sun, the stronger ram gets his lady.

Yet, as John wrote in *Christian Herald* (June 1987), cooperation is more essential to our survival than competition, particularly between a husband and wife. A swimming coach who works with handicapped children added this insight.

"I know I'm getting somewhere," the coach said, "on

the day a youngster stops comparing himself with some-body else."

A normal child, he explained, could swim to the end of the pool and back in the time it might take a handicapped child just to get down the steps. Equal concentration and effort were required in both instances. "The trick," the coach said, "is to get my kids to take their eyes off the next guy. Instead, each youngster has to learn to compete with the best in himself. I tell him he then belongs to the Special Order of Competitors."

The coach's insight has application beyond the pool-side. It is wisdom for all of us who are scrappers by nature but find ourselves in a situation such as marriage, where outdoing the other person is not appropriate. We are prob-ably never going to eliminate our competitive streak. But we can *transform* it.

John still considers himself a competitive person, but he is learning to redirect that energy so it becomes a force for improving his own performance, rather than begrudging someone else's.

He came upon a Bible quotation that sums up the changed perspective that has helped him so much.

"Each one," wrote Paul, "should test his own actions. Then he can take pride in himself, without comparing himself to someone else" (see Galatians 6:4).

Paul's main enemy wasn't the Pharisees or Roman offi-cials; his chief antagonist was a dark entity, the enemy Satan himself. The main battleground was inside Paul. That is where he won or lost. That is where we win or lose.

One of Paul's statements is used today by coaches, ath-letes, organizations as a rallying point:

> The one thing I do . . . is to forget what is behind me
> and do my best to reach what is ahead. So I run
> straight toward the goal in order to win the prize,
> which is God's call through Christ Jesus to the life
> above.
>
> Philippians 3:13–14, GNB

The prize Paul refers to of life everlasting far transcends
any medal or award or honor we can achieve in this world.

Being a Real Man

More good news. There are organizations that are positive forces on the negative sports scene. The Fellowship
of Christian Athletes since the early 1950s has had a cen-
tral role in transforming young people's lives, including
two in our family.

More recently, Athletes in Action has made an impact
on the athletic world with its emphasis on evangelism.

Another vital organization, Manhood, Inc., held a meeting not so long ago at the Sheraton Hotel just outside of
Washington, D.C., that helped put it all in perspective for
me. It was scheduled for a warm Saturday in June from 9
A.M. to 3 P.M.

"How many men will give up a sunny Saturday to sit for
six hours at a conference?" I asked myself. "They'll be
lucky to get fifty men there."

Wrong. Some 1,500 men, mostly under forty, jammed
the main ballroom of the Sheraton. As the hordes poured
in I stared at them in a state of shock.

Then I looked at the man whose ministry had drawn
them. Was he some kind of rock singer turned evangeli-

cal? No—Edwin Louis Cole is a balding man close to seventy. And he certainly is no "cool cat." But what drive and enthusiasm!

"We're here to praise the Lord!" he shouted. "We're here to show each other how much we love the Lord! I'm so tired of seeing those milquetoast, limp-wristed, morally destitute, whining men who will not face up to the responsibilities God has given them. Remember this—being male is a matter of birth; being a man is a matter of your choice."

The singing was fantastic. Fifteen hundred male voices sounded like a heavenly choir as they exploded with "Our God Reigns!"

Ed Cole knows where men are most vulnerable: sex, money, communication. He ripped open all the male defenses, deception, phoniness and soon got hundreds to stand who wanted to be freed of their bondages. Then a spontaneous prayer time began.

"Don't pray for God to perform some kind of supernatural miracle in your lives," Ed told them. "Pray for wisdom. It's wisdom that will give you the strategy to win the victory over what enslaves you. And it doesn't happen in one hour or one day. You work at it, every day."

Then he had all the men repeat the key phrases.

"Tell your wife you love her. How often do you do this?"

"Every day!" came the thunderous response.

"How often do you pray?"

"Every day!"

"Read the Bible?"

"Every day!"

At different points during this six-hour get-together (less

a 45-minute lunch break), Ed Cole summoned a young man named Bob Andrews to the stage. Bob has a praise ministry in Indiana that focuses on two words, *Go, Jesus.* He also has a gift for rallying the troops.

And then it happened. For the first time in my life I saw and heard men at a religious gathering stand up and shout and wave their arms and pound one another on the back and explode with ear-splitting applause as they would at a sports event.

I felt a new high myself. We men have this basic drive, this competitiveness, inside us. How great to see it channeled for God!

Questions for Reflection

1) Where do you feel the main competition is in your life?
2) Has competition been beneficial or harmful to you?
3) When is competition good? When is it bad?
4) Do you see Jesus as a competitor? If yes, in what way?
5) What does the prize Paul refers to in his Philippians quote mean to you? Is it your goal?

11
Brother

Am I my brother's keeper?

Genesis 4:9, KJV

They were young men and brothers. They both owned land; one was a farmer and the other raised sheep.

They both also knew God.

To pay tribute to their Lord, each brother brought Him an offering. Cain gathered some produce off his land and offered it up to God. Abel did much better. He brought to God the very best of his flock.

God was pleased with Abel's sacrificial spirit and told him so. He was not impressed with what Cain had brought Him.

This angered Cain so much he brooded. Jealous feelings stabbed him. Then he boiled over, stalked his brother in the field and killed him.

The Lord said to Cain, "Where is Abel your brother?"

Cain, still angry and now feeling guilty, answered with a plaintive cry that has echoed down through the ages: "Am I my brother's keeper?"

Scripture does not record God's answer. But we know He expects us to be good brothers to our siblings and to be concerned for other men and women in a brotherly way.

What is a brother?

The dictionary says: A brother is "a male having the same mother and father as another . . . one who shares a common ancestry, allegiance or purpose with another (as in a fraternity or lodge) . . . a close male friend . . . a member of a men's religious order."

When Brothers Fall Out

A good brother is a loving brother. Yet often this love can be put to terrible tests. Take the De Klerk brothers in South Africa: F.W. and Willem.

F.W. De Klerk, the president of South Africa, belongs to the National Party, which has long championed the apartheid policy of racism.

Sitting only a few feet behind F.W. De Klerk on inauguration day in September 1989 was a leader of the opposition to apartheid and also his brother, Willem De Klerk, eight years older.

Despite this *broedertivis* (Afrikaans for a brotherly falling out) F.W. and Willem have great affection for each other. They see each other regularly and good-naturedly try to win each other to their point of view. The De Klerk family tree is rooted mostly in conservative politics. Willem began veering leftward while editing a Christian paper in the 1950s and soon began to speak out against apartheid.

Their differences came to a head late in 1989 as F.W. tried to work out a compromise in his troubled nation,

197

giving blacks the right to vote, but safeguarding white rights, such as segregated schools and neighborhoods. Willem opposed any segregation.

Then early in 1990 F.W. De Klerk freed Nelson Mandela, black anti-apartheid leader, who had been imprisoned for 27 years for anti-government activities. The world applauded, but far right conservatives in F.W. De Klerk's party were angry. Was the leftist Willem De Klerk winning over his conservative brother?

The story of brother versus brother in South African politics intrigues not only everyone in this volatile nation, but the whole world as well.

Ever since Cain slew Abel, brothers have vied with each other, sometimes fought each other. It is a test of a man's strength that he can remain a good brother despite *broedertivis*.

John Edgar Wideman is a professor of English at the University of Wyoming, the author of six works of highly acclaimed fiction, including *Sent for You Yesterday*, which won the prestigious Pen/Faulkner award in 1984. Professor Wideman is black, married and the father of three. He is also the brother of Robert Douglas Wideman, ten years younger, who was involved in a theft that resulted in a killing near Pittsburgh, Pennsylvania. Rob was sentenced to life imprisonment without possibility of probation or parole.

Until this tragedy John and Rob had not been close. When Rob was sentenced, John had to face the question, "Am I my brother's keeper?" He went through some deep soul-searching before he decided yes, he was.

John began by trying to think through such questions as "Why is Rob there behind bars? Why me here, successful in academe and in my writing? We both came from a good home with loving parents."

He recalled his mother's description of her young son: "That Robby . . . he wakes up in the morning looking for a party. Up there under the covers he's thinking, Where is it today? Where's the fun?"

Good seed, bad seed—that seemed such an oversimplification. Rob had all the potential to be as solid and respected as his older brother. The choices he made led to his life imprisonment.

John could have distanced himself from his imprisoned brother. Because of his family and university responsibilities, visits to Rob could be only occasional. After much thought, John chose instead to build a new relationship with Rob through correspondence. Not just a letter every now and then, but regular letters back and forth that could even be the basis for a book. Letters that John hoped try to uncover why Rob did what he did. Letters that John hoped might help rebuild and recreate a lost person.

At the beginning there were obstacles to overcome between the brother who had it all and the brother who had lost it all. John prayed that Rob's sentence would be reduced. It didn't happen. So he prayed for a change in Robby that would help him rise above his surroundings. That did happen.

Years passed. Letters between the brothers continued. Rob had times of abject despair, times of hope. Gradually he began to show more inner strength. He achieved an inner calm, a degree of self-sufficiency and self-reliance never apparent when he was running the streets. In some unexplainable way he had grown accustomed to that which was unbearable—imprisonment. He had named it, tamed it.

The time came when Rob enrolled in the prison school. Rough going. There was the math he never had in high school. Hours relearning being a student. Meanwhile he took a part-time job in the prison hospital.

The love of his family was constant, the words of brother John always before him. Rob hung in there, not only graduating but serving as the main speaker at the prison graduation ceremony. His mother attended and reported that her son looked marvelous decked out in cap and gown. "He was eloquent, like a preacher, had the audience clapping and rocking in their seats." Here are excerpts from Rob's speech:

> I am serving a life sentence of which I have served seven years plus. I mention it only to show that even someone with as bleak a future as mine can still strive to better his condition by bettering himself through education.
>
> I hope that my example will help my fellow prisoners to strive for their own self-attainment. I hope that they can look at me and say, "Well, if he can do it with no guarantee that he will ever have the chance to pursue all of his goals, then why can't I?" And if through my example some of society's outcasts will find the willpower to pull their lives back together and become productive citizens instead of social burdens, then I will have performed a very worthwhile task.
>
> My prayer is that the Bureau of Corrections will see that they do society an injustice when they imprison men for two or five or ten years without demanding

of these men that they at least learn a vocation before
they can be released.

It is doubtful that Rob would have achieved what he did
in prison without his brother's love and concern. The letters between them did result in a book, *Brothers and Keepers*
by John Edgar Wideman, telling the story of what it meant
to fulfill God's commandment to be his brother's keeper.

A man shows inner strength by being a good brother.
He may not agree with his brother's politics (the De
Klerks), or his brother's lifestyle (the Widemans), and he
may not even like his brothers or sisters, but he has a
responsibility to care for them. Caring for them does not
necessarily mean taking care of them, but loving them.
God often requires us to love the unlovable.

How does a brother do that?

I don't think we can will ourselves to love this way. I can
say to myself, "I know I should love my brother, but I just
can't stand him. He's so obnoxious. But I'll try."

It won't work. I can generate some affection this way,
but it won't last. Human effort can achieve a lot, but it
can't produce love when there's hate, or disgust, or total
apathy. But love can come in a supernatural way through
me to the person I loathe.

Loving the Unlovable

I met Jim Spencer in a church Bible study class, learned
his story through class discussion and talking with him
personally. In high school and college Jim's flowing blond
hair, good looks and athletic ability won him the label
"Golden Boy." His two younger sisters, Janet and Julie,

were surprising opposites. Janet, the older, was a straight arrow from childhood. She was gifted in music, academics, sports; everyone loved her. Julie, the younger, was not attractive, nor very talented. She became a rebel in her teens, had trouble making friends.

The Spencer family was middle-class respectable (the father a dentist, the mother a part-time schoolteacher). In 1968 Julie left home at age eighteen to live with a disreputable town character. The whole Spencer family was traumatized. When Julie became a part of a "hippie" community with her long hair, granny glasses, jeans and sandals, the Spencer family recoiled even more.

Julie's parents continued communication with her as best they could, but Jim "wrote off" his sister. The Golden Boy became a successful architect, married and moved to another state. For years he had no contact at all with Julie. Meanwhile Jim became active in our local church.

The change in Jim began during the adult Bible class. The course: Family Relationships. There were sessions on being a father, a husband, a wife, a son or daughter. Then came one on being a good brother or sister.

"We don't hear much about the vital role brothers and sisters have in our family system," the teacher said. "Too bad. We read about so many lost people today because their parents failed them. Divorce, negligent fathers, single parent mothers . . . they're epidemic. You know what? There are negligent, cop-out brothers, too, who could have made a difference."

Most of us in the class related to this. Jim especially.

"If you're one of those cop-out brothers or sisters, it's never too late to change," the teacher continued. "First, examine your heart. Why did you break off a relationship with your sibling? Was it jealousy? Did he hurt you badly when you were children together? Did she embarrass you?"

There it is! thought Jim. Julie was an embarrassment to the family. He didn't like the way she looked, or talked, or acted. She was a mess.

"Go back in years," the teacher continued. "Was there a time when you and your sibling enjoyed being together? What did you like about him? When did things change with her?"

Jim's thoughts retraced the years. He liked Julie before her teens. She was cute. Fun. As a teenager she changed. She began running around with oddballs, wearing awful-looking clothes; then it was alcohol and drugs.

"Let's assume you want to rediscover your brother or your sister," the teacher went on. "How do you do it?" Long pause. "Are you with me? If this applies to you in any way, raise your hands."

Almost all the hands went up.

"O.K. A journey begins with the first step. Don't go right into some kind of confrontation. Pray about it. Ask the Lord to show you where *you've* been wrong. Develop a strategy. Should you write a letter? Make a telephone call? Perhaps a visit? Maybe you should discuss it first with your parents. Rebuilding a broken or damaged relationship takes time."

The teacher then used the story of Jacob and Esau to show what Jacob had to do to restore things with his brother whose birthright he had stolen (Genesis 25, 27).

Jim Spencer began the long journey of reconciliation

with his sister Julie. It was slow going. Julie scorned his first efforts on the telephone.

"Why are you calling me, Jim? We've nothing in common."

"We're brother and sister."

"What does that mean?"

"I'm not sure I know. But we can't just ignore each other."

Julie grunted. "We have for years."

"I'd like to change that. May I come and see you?"

"No. I don't want you coming here." Pause. "You represent all the things we're opposed to in this community."

"Like what?"

"Like middle-class WASP hypocrisy and phoniness."

Jim bit his lip to stifle an angry retort. "Where and when can I see you?"

"At Mom and Dad's. I'll be there in two weeks."

While talking to his parents about coming home Jim learned from his father two sad facts. Julie was an alcoholic. Julie had also tried to commit suicide two months before. She had taken an overdose of sleeping pills; an ambulance had been called in time. Julie hadn't told her parents. The news had come from the hospital where Julie had been in and out overnight.

When Jim finally did sit down alone with his sister, he was dismayed all over again at her appearance. In her mid-twenties now, she looked many years older. She was gaunt, unkempt, haggard, miserable. *How do I talk to this person?* Jim asked himself.

The small talk was limp, painful. Jim struggled to be upbeat. Julie would stare at him for a while, then look down.

"Why did you try to end your life?" he finally asked.

She glared at him without answering.

"Why? . . . Why? . . . Why?" he asked again.

"Because I'm worthless," she finally answered.

"You're not worthless. You're . . . you're one of God's special children."

Julie's look was disdainful. "So my brother's got religion. Is that why you've taken an interest in me?"

Jim didn't know how to answer that one. "I came here because . . . well, because I care about you, Julie."

Julie shook her head. "You never showed it. You were the Golden Boy. Good things always happened to you. I was just an embarrassment to you—and Janet."

"Your sister loves you."

"She has a funny way of showing it."

"So we've been selfish and insensitive. You went your way; we went ours."

For the first time tears appeared in Julie's eyes. "I couldn't do anything right. You and Janet did everything right. Do you know what it's like to have a brother and sister like that? I was so ordinary I began to hate myself. Then I got to the point where I just didn't want to live. I felt completely worthless. You can't understand that, can you, Jim?"

Tears filled her brother's eyes. "No, I can't. And I don't believe you're worthless. God gives each one of us a special gift or talent. Sometimes more than one. There is something of great worth in you, Julie. You'll find it."

Julie was persuaded to go into an alcoholic treatment center. Jim began to pray daily for his sister and also to write her encouraging notes. And then he got his Bible study class to take Julie on as a special prayer project.

A week after Julie came out of treatment, she wrote Jim.

"Surprise . . . I was invited back to tell my story to the new class of recovering alcoholics. . . . I've also become active in Alcoholics Anonymous."

Two weeks later another note from Janet. "I'm doing a lot of speaking at treatment centers and support groups. And another surprise . . . I'm pretty good at it!"

A telephone call to Jim's parents confirmed Julie's progress. "You wouldn't recognize your sister. She's cut her hair, bought new clothes, been fitted for contacts. The change is amazing!"

A month later Julie got a job in the public relations office of a firm that was establishing rehab centers throughout the state for alcohol and drug addicts. Julie had found her special gift.

A key factor in Julie's change was her brother's decision to be a real brother to her and his discovery that he could love the unlovable—until she became lovable.

Giving More Time

The chemistry between siblings has always been volatile and unpredictable. Not much has been written about these situations, probably because they don't have the generational impact that the father-wife, father-son, motherdaughter relationships have.

I was convicted by Jim Spencer's story. During my selfcentered teens, twenties and thirties, I paid but nominal attention to my sister, Pat, who is seven years younger. We lived in different sections of the country, had different interests. We kept in touch, but there was little confiding in each other. Pat is a creative, strong-willed woman like our mother. I have both resisted and been drawn to this type.

Pat married and had three daughters. One died in her teens. Another was the solid, dependable type. The third got involved with drugs and alcohol, had a dramatic turn-around and became another gifted, strong-willed woman. She now has two children.

As with Jim Spencer, God convicted me about my sister. He showed me that I had an important responsibility not only to her, but also to my nieces. My sin here was neglect, indifference, lack of a caring heart.

Early on I had attempted to persuade my sister to believe about religion as I did. She wasn't buying. "You have your beliefs, I have mine," she told me. So we drifted apart. When her daughter became an addict, I examined my responsibilities as an uncle. If the brother's accountability has not been clearly expounded by preachers and writers, the uncle's role is totally vague.

As I prayed about it, I received several bits of guidance. My use of time. A lot of selfishness here. That had to change. A new commitment was in order.

"Lord," I prayed, "back in 1948 I gave my life to You. Perhaps I didn't realize then that this included a gift to You of all the time I had left. I confess I have been jealous of my time, using lots of it for the things I want to do, things that have nothing to do with You at all. I see this as wrong, Lord. So now I make available to You all my time to use as You see fit. Each day I will ask for Your instructions about this."

This was an important step for me to take. It dissolved something hard and selfish inside me. Sometimes I drift back into old habits, but today Sandy knows about this commitment and will remind me of it if necessary.

I am a better brother because of it. A better uncle, too. And I'm learning how to be a brother in a larger sense, too. For we are all called to a brotherhood relationship in which our love for all others is not an *eros* or sexual or selfish kind of love, but *agape* or a brotherly love that gives unselfishly and asks nothing in return.

Graham Pulkingham, Episcopal pastor and author, once preached a sermon called "My Brother Betty" in which he stated that he loved his wife, Betty, one way as a husband, but he also had a brotherly love for her that transcended the physical.

When I asked Graham to explain this in more detail, he wrote me as follows: "Christ's love through me loves my wife, Betty, in exactly the same way He does every person for whom He died. Since Betty and I are both *in Him*, Christ's *agape* works in her to love me, and Christ's *agape* works in me to love her. It is Christ in my wife that I love above all else.

"This does not mean there is no extraordinary affection in my relationship with Betty. *Philia*—tender, heartwarming, intimate love—is a blessed part of our marital life. And erotic love *eros* is also there, as evidenced by our brood of six children. But *agape* will not allow me to choose love for Betty above Christ's love for others; rather *agape* compels me to choose to love the world for which Love died."

Thus a man can go far beyond being a good brother to other brothers and sisters in his family; he can be an *agape*-type brother to all other members of his family, plus friends, neighbors, co-workers, even strangers. To do this he follows the example of Jesus' unconditional love for all mankind. But being a good brother doesn't come naturally.

Why not?

Does it go back to Cain and Abel?

Did the fit of jealousy that compelled Cain to murder his brother become a bad seed passed down from man to man, generation after generation, decade after decade, century after century?

There is certainly no need for such generational bondage. A Man was born of humble parents some 2,000 years ago who broke any such bonds. His message was love; He stated that man could perform no greater act of love than to give his life for a brother. This Man preached it—and then lived it.

Questions for Reflection

1) What is the best kind of brother-to-brother relationship?
2) What is the best kind of brother-to-sister relationship?
3) Can you list five brother relationships in the Bible that were tense or worse? (See below.)
4) What was the relationship between Jesus and His brothers and sisters? Did Jesus explain this in Scripture?
5) How does a husband have an *agape* (brotherly) relationship with his wife? With his neighbor? With a stranger?

Answers to Question 3:

5) Moses and Aaron
4) Ham and Shem and Japheth
3) Joseph and his brothers
2) Esau and Jacob
1) Cain and Abel

12
Churchman

Is any sick among you? let him call for the elders of
the church; and let them pray over him, anointing
him with oil in the name of the Lord.

James 5:14, KJV

As we walked down the hospital corridor, I tried to
think through the ritual I was about to perform. It would
be a new experience for me, this laying on of hands to the
sick. I felt inadequate and realized my awkwardness
would be obvious.

"Do you have the olive oil?" I asked my stepson Peter
Marshall.

"Jamie has it."

Jamie Buckingham reached into his coat pocket and
handed me a small bottle containing the clear oil.

Children's Hospital in Boston is one of the best in the
world for handling the wide variety of diseases that strike
down the young. When Amy Catherine Marshall was born
on July 22, 1971, the diagnosis was grim: genetic disorders
involving the liver, kidneys and brain.

Peter and Edith Marshall, her parents, and Catherine
and I as grandparents decided to battle this negative prog-

nosis the only way we knew. We asked twelve others to join us at Orleans, Massachusetts, for four days of intensive prayer. The story has been told in detail in Catherine Marshall's *Light in My Darkest Night*. I relate a single episode here to disclose its impact on me as a man and as an elder of the church.

For I had been chosen this day to anoint tiny Amy Catherine with oil, based on James 5:14.

Amy Catherine was in a special ward on the fifth floor of the hospital. Before going up to her room, Peter, Jamie and I stopped to pray in the small hospital chapel.

Upstairs in her room Peter held Amy Catherine while I took the cap off the bottle and poured some oil on my fingers. Then I took the baby in my arms. She was so tiny and helpless, I felt tears gather behind my eyelids. We were not there to question the why of these ailments, I told myself, but to ask for a healing. Yes, even to claim a miracle!

We stood with Amy Catherine in the corner of the room, which was open to a larger ward where a number of infants lay ill in small cribs. Two nurses from this outer room looked at us curiously.

Holding Amy Catherine in the crook of my left arm, I gently rubbed the oil over her forehead. The eyes fluttered open for a moment, then closed. My prayer was halting, uncertain. "Lord, I'm an imperfect instrument for this kind of thing. But I believe in Your power. So we've come here to ask You to heal this tiny baby. The doctors say there is no hope. . . . With You, Lord, there is always hope. Use my hands and my prayer, Lord. We ask for a miracle."

Peter added a prayer of his own. We each kissed the

baby, one of the nurses came up, took the infant from us and placed her back in the crib.

When Amy Catherine slipped away after only six weeks of life, it seemed like a total defeat. Were all our prayers for nothing? Then the tally sheet began to come in on the number of people this infant had ministered to. There were some startling healings in the lives of the sixteen people who had come to pray, also among several in Peter's church.

Taking Authority

My role as an elder during the short, intense drama of Amy Catherine's life seemed at the time a somewhat faltering one. Yet something important happened in my spirit. Men like doing what they do well and duck activity where they feel uncomfortable or unskilled. In this situation I had moved from uncertain ground to a position of authority on pure faith, overcoming a fear in the process. The Lord had honored that.

I have been involved in various kinds of church activity since 1949, the greater part of it attending meetings, planning programs and dealing with church business. Admittedly, these are all necessary functions. Still, when they absorb ninety percent or more of your time as a churchman, something is wrong. Concerned about this soon after the Amy Catherine experience, I started probing into the meaning and historical significance of the church elder.

Webster's dictionary was my first stop. It defines *elder* as "a senior person," one who is "given special functions or authority consistent with his age, experience, or dignity, a layman who shares with the minister the government of the church." Although different churches use different terms, a church elder, I concluded, was one with definite spiritual and legal responsibilities.

From our library I pulled out an old copy of *The Book of Church Order*, containing the constitution of the Presbyterian Church in the United States. The duties it outlined of a ruling elder, as adopted by the General Assembly of 1876, fascinated me:

Those elders were to possess the same authority in the church as the ministers of the Word. They were to "cultivate zealously an aptitude to teach the Bible," be able to supply religious services to any mission point or church where there was no pastor. "By the holiness of their walk," elders were to be an example to the flock. Together with the pastor, elders were "to exercise church government and discipline."

In fact, elders were specifically told that they were to watch diligently over the flock and "correct by private admonition those individuals who had bad attitudes, were involved in wrongdoing, or anything that is harmful to the church." Elders were "to pray with and for the people, visit in their homes, especially the sick; they were to seek diligently the fruit of the preached Word among the flock."

When I read these duties to the other elders of our church in Delray Beach, Florida, there was silence, a blank look on most faces. None had ever gone to the home of the sick to pray and anoint them with oil. None had ever taught a Bible class. The idea that they should correct members of the congregation for wrong behavior repelled them. "It just isn't done today," said one.

In fact, the pastor had not encouraged his laymen to

take spiritual leadership in the church. He saw his elders as a church management team, handling business matters while he took over all spiritual leadership functions. By doing this he blocked his elders from the growth they needed to better serve the congregation.

Something had happened to me during the crisis with Amy Catherine that made me, as a man, dissatisfied with such a passive role in the church. In time Catherine and I encountered a pastor, George Callahan, who left a thriving Presbyterian Church in Narberth, Pennsylvania, to come to south Florida and begin a new work patterned on the book of Acts.

In 1977 the New Covenant Church of Pompano Beach was the result. I was one of the founding elders, Catherine a key Bible teacher, intercessor, encourager. We elders were all given small vials of oil and trained in the laying-on-of-hands prayer for healing. For the first five years services were held in a school auditorium.

Laymen had to be ready for any situation during the two-hour service. The pastor might call upon you to pray, make the announcements, give a testimony. What a contrast to my previous church experience!

Once a teenage mother brought her infant son to the altar for baptism. Then she testified that she was unmarried and had been "rescued from drugs by my Savior."

At this point we elders of the church came forward and knelt beside the mother and child while the baby was offered up to the Lord. Then the pastor made it clear that both mother and child were now a very special responsibility of the church. Following the service, several people came to the mother with specific offers of clothing, food and infant care.

After every service, we elders circulated through the audience, offering a word of encouragement here, not hesitating to counsel or even correct our people as the situation demanded. Several times an elder stopped a conversation to pray aloud on the spot for the specific need. A woman and her husband approached me to ask for prayer.

"We have been childless now for eight years," she said. "Would you ask the Lord to bless us that we might be able to have a baby?"

As if I had done this sort of thing all my life, I steered the couple away from the noisy conversations about us, placed my hands on each of them, and prayed, "Lord, You alone know the reason why this couple hasn't been able to have a child. We ask right now for a healing of any deformity or disorder or problem that blocks Your natural process of conception and birth. Bless this marriage. Thank You for Your gift of life." I never found out what happened, but the role of the intercessor is to pray and not worry about the results.

New Covenant Church met the people where they were, began a healing and counseling institute, set up a food pantry and shop where food and clothing could be obtained at cost, or no cost. Today New Covenant has nearly 1,500 members, gives tens of thousands of dollars yearly to causes all over the world. Most important, it ministers to the deep needs of the whole community.

Today in many churches men are given assignments that are unchallenging and routine. We are too often chosen as leaders because of our community standing or financial knowledge, not because of any spiritual gifts we might have. Fortunately, this situation is beginning to change in many churches: Old stereotyped church machinery is being revamped to let the fresh wind of the Holy Spirit move more freely.

Women in the Church

Historically and scripturally Church elders have been men. Today more and more women have become leaders in the Church, and rightly so since they have special gifts. A number of denominations have women pastors. There are strong differences about this between Church purists who say that Christ by not including women among His disciples set the permanent example for Church leadership, and the realists who say that the Church needs the vitality and leadership that women can give.

I can understand both viewpoints. Without strong male leadership, church membership declines and the power goes out of it. Yet I have seen arrogant, domineering men stifle the creativity of a church and bring about a seething discontent.

One woman who warns other women about taking a too dominant role in church situations is Virginia Lively, an Episcopalian with special gifts in healing and teaching. Always she makes two points: (1) men need to assume their scriptural roles as heads of their homes, and (2) a church will grow only when its men exert strong leadership. This last issue came to a head some years ago at a Florida church when its pastor invited Virginia to participate in the leadership of a weekend retreat for about twenty key couples.

The pastor was having difficulty getting men to attend services and church affairs, much less take leadership. He had discovered that his church women were more responsive to the spiritual life. They had started prayer groups, bought most of the religious books, were the ones who attended meetings. Women filled the teaching roles in Sunday school programs and other responsible positions because men refused to become involved.

When this particular weekend conference began on Friday night with a sharing session, Virginia noted right away that the women were doing most of the talking while the men were looking at their watches. Church elders (*vestrymen* in the Episcopal Church) seemed uncomfortable away from their familiar roles as ushers or handlers of church business and finances.

Virginia Lively opened the Saturday morning meeting with a startling proposal. "I suggest that all women in this room keep quiet for the duration of this morning session. We want to listen to you men. Tell us what Christ is doing in your lives. Tell us how you receive guidance on your jobs from the Holy Spirit. Tell us how you see God at work in your families."

As the pastor took over the meeting, there was an embarrassed silence. Finally Harvey, a tall, distinguished-looking vestryman, stood up. "You are asking me to be a part of something here for which I feel totally unqualified. I know how to run my business and as an employer I deal with all kinds of people. I can serve this church as an usher on Sunday and as a trustee in charge of development. If you give me a topic and time for preparation, I can give a speech to the church congregation. But when you ask me to let the Holy Spirit run my business, my home, my whole life—well, frankly, this scares me to death. I just don't have that kind of relationship with the Lord."

"Would you like to?" asked the pastor.

Harvey was thoughtful for a long moment. "I admit there are times when I feel an intense inner loneliness, when I wonder what life is all about, really. My wife has found something in the church that has changed her. I admire this. But I resist change. To ask God to take over my life, well, frankly, that's hard for a man in my situation to do."

Another vestryman picked it up. "Harvey speaks for many of us men here, I'm sure. When it comes to finances or church property or building a new sanctuary, I'll pitch right in. But to talk about my spiritual life, or pray aloud, or relate Scripture to my business—I guess I'm a private person."

"But can we leaders of the church be private persons in regard to our faith?" continued the pastor. "One of the purposes of this get-together is to try to find out what spiritual gifts we have. Women seem to be the more articulate ones, so we're asking them to be silent this morning to give you men a chance to speak up."

"Frankly, I was dreading this weekend," Joe, a foreman at a local plant, spoke out. "To spend two whole days talking about religion and seeking God's guidance for our lives seemed such a waste of time."

"Do you feel any different about it now?" asked the pastor.

"I think we're getting honest," he continued. "I frankly resented the pressure put on me to come this weekend. There's a football game I had to miss. And I knew the women would try to take over because they always do in this church."

"Let me be honest for a moment," the pastor put in. "Women tend to dominate this church for one reason: You men let them. You let them by your absence and your silence. Because of this I feel a great sense of failure. I can't get you men to take on spiritual responsibilities. Understand now—I'm grateful for the way you take charge of the financial and physical needs of our church. This is important. But it isn't enough. A church is not alive and vital unless the laymen are on fire for the Lord. I'm tired of my efforts to whip up something among you men. It doesn't work. I don't think it ever has or will. The Lord has to do it. So I'm stating here and now that I admit my failures and I'm asking the Holy Spirit to take over my life and our church."

Tears filled the pastor's eyes and he stopped. Then he closed this session with prayer.

The Men Take Over

New feelings began to stir inside the men the rest of that Saturday. Several went for long walks to think things over. Some went alone to the altar to pray. At a Communion service that night couples knelt, held hands, served the elements to each other. At the final Sunday morning meeting the atmosphere was changed.

A softspoken man said quietly, "Last night I felt the Lord showing me something, but I was too shy to speak out. This morning I will. I have allowed my wife to take charge of the spiritual life of our home during all of our marriage, and I see that this is wrong. Right here and now

219

I ask the Lord's forgiveness. From now on I intend to be the head of our home as Christ is head of the Church."

"Praise the Lord!" came an involuntary cry from the man's wife. Then she stood up suddenly. "I know I'm supposed to shut up. But I just want to say one sentence. If you men will take charge, I'll be happy and quiet as a clam."

Laughter broke the tension. Then, like water spilling through an ever-widening crack in a dam, man after man stood up to admit fears, failure, inadequacy and hunger for God's power. One said, "I've never prayed aloud in my life and the Lord just told me to do so." Then in halting words, but with moving intensity, he poured out his heart to God. Next to him his wife wept.

The whole tone of the meeting now switched from talk to prayer as the Spirit flowed through these formerly reserved, somewhat antagonistic males. A confession, a word of praise, an impassioned pledge to change old habits, a simple vow to be a better husband followed one after the other. Most of the women now had their handkerchiefs out.

As a climax one man stood up and said quietly, "Lord, I feel I've been given the music and words of a song." When he opened his mouth, expressions of love and joy poured forth in such melodic sweetness that there was a feeling of being in the presence of angels.

Awed, the men and women sat silent as the Spirit warmed cold hearts, touched emotions, rekindled the dead embers of love, healed wounds of bitterness and resentment, and reduced haughty hearts to the humility of children before the Father.

Thus did the men in this church get started toward becoming vestrymen in the true sense. The Spirit of God swept through this group of people, lives were changed, men and women found their proper roles, and the work of the Lord surged forward.

Man's desire to be in control either keeps him away from the church or keeps the church away from God. The Florida vestryman summed it up when he said he would serve the church when he could do it his way: Handle business matters with which he was familiar, prepare and deliver a talk in the manner to which he was accustomed. But don't ask him to relinquish control to a God he could not see who would tell him how to live his life.

Almost all men in the church face this issue. They want to pick and choose the functions they feel comfortable doing, rather than allow the pastor or others to assign them to places where the need is greatest.

Ideally, each man should be given a job that will stretch him. The one who feels shy about praying aloud should be told that this is his growing edge and so to be prepared to be called upon. I have watched men struggle with this and did myself in the early years of my church life. We men duck doing things we're not good at. Prayers don't have to be eloquent—just from the heart. The best training place for spoken prayers is one's home.

Certain church jobs, however, require people with gifts: teaching, preaching, administration, bookkeeping. Men (and women, too) should earn the right to do these jobs. A man could develop a teaching gift by first handling a Sunday school class.

It all comes down to the way a man views his church life. Does he choose a church where he can give of himself, or one where he just receives? Some men will have to battle an innate selfishness, a placid nature that wants to be a spectator rather than a participant.

Jesus faced these problems with men when He chose the Twelve. Even after three years under the Master's teaching, the disciples didn't understand much of what He was saying. They were jealous of each other, sought special considerations, were incapable of strong loyalty. Jesus was quite aware of these weaknesses when He chose them.

The disciples thought that Jesus was preparing to set up a kingdom on earth. Jesus had something much bigger in mind, with each one of His "weak" Twelve to play a specific part in it.

Questions for Reflection

1) How does a pastor maintain strong leadership in his church and still develop spiritual leadership among his men?
2) How can women best serve the Church today?
3) What can be done to bring out men's spiritual gifts? Women's?
4) How does the James 5:14 passage apply to your church?
5) Are you satisfied with the way leaders are chosen/elected in your church?

13
Thawing the Frozen Male

Therefore I take pleasure in infirmities, in reproaches,
in necessities, in persecutions, in distresses for
Christ's sake: for when I am weak, then am I strong.
2 Corinthians 12:10, KJV

The men begin to arrive a little after seven this Saturday
morning. The coffee machine is turned on, rolls and
doughnuts set forth. Seventy-plus chairs are placed in a
circle, printed nametags laid out on the table.

This men's group of New Covenant Church in Pompano Beach has been meeting every Saturday now in this
large classroom for over two years. I attend whenever I am
in Florida because this is my home church, because I am
challenged by men's groups, but also because the men in
this group are so open and honest that they always minister to me.

This Saturday many of those on hand are hurting. A
number have physical ailments. A few are recovering addicts. Several need to go to treatment. Some are estranged
from their wives. Their ages range from college student to
white-haired retiree; they are a mixture of whites, blacks,
Hispanics and other nationalities.

"What do you want to sing?" George Callahan, the feisty, multi-talented pastor smiles as he greets "his boys." His Irish voice leads them off in a praise verse. How these men sing!

The sharing begins. A middle-aged man in a yellow T-shirt rises to his feet. "I leave tomorrow for Dunklin. Six months treatment. Thanks for hanging in there with me." Tears fill his eyes and he sits down. The man next to him puts an arm around his shoulder.

And so it goes. One by one they stand, give their names (there are always newcomers attending) and report. One young man tells of a reconciliation with his wife, another how the Lord has prospered his business, another how he's persuaded an unbelieving son to attend church.

A gray-haired man stands up. Softspoken, I figure him for an accountant. "I'm fifty years old, been a Christian now for four years. Before that I served time."

He takes his glasses off, wipes them to get control of himself.

"Today I have a good business. An honest business. I'm clean and it feels wonderful. My family has stuck with me—they've been great. Several days ago a government official asked me questions about one of my old operations back in the 1970s. I told him the truth—even though it could cost me dearly."

He takes out his Bible. "Here is some Scripture that sums up my story," he concludes, and reads Romans 6:20–23:

> In those days when you were slaves of sin you didn't bother much with goodness. And what was the result? Evidently not good, since you are ashamed now

even to think about those things you used to do, for all of them end in eternal doom. But now you are free from the power of sin and are slaves of God, and his benefits to you include holiness and everlasting life. For the wages of sin is death, but the free gift of God is eternal life.

(LB)

I've thought a lot about that fifty-year-old man since that Saturday morning. Most would label him a weak man. At one point he certainly was. But not today. He has his family together, his integrity, a solid business and the faith to face the consequences of his actions rather than running away.

Strong men . . . weak men. Hard to tell them apart at times. So many of the supposedly strong ones have glaring weaknesses; and those that seem weak on the outside can be tough underneath.

Two Sides of Man

I mentioned earlier the two natures in men—masculine and feminine, complementary poles within each human psyche. The two need to be in balance for the man to be fulfilled, complete.

If the masculine side dominates too much the man becomes aggressive, abusive, predatory. He enjoys women as conquests, is poor husband and father material. If the feminine side in a man dominates he will be more artistic, gentle, tenderhearted, weak, submissive, effeminate.

Ernest Hemingway was admired for his macho lifestyle. Pete Rose wore the label "indestructible man." Babe Ruth

225

was the "King of Swat." Hemingway, Ruth and Rose were superstars, yet tragic figures after their glory years. Strong men on the surface because of their masculine images. Yet how strong were they?

All three failed miserably as husbands, Rose and Hemingway as fathers.

All three failed at self-control. We somehow want to excuse the excesses of alcohol, drugs, gambling, immorality in people we admire; or we don't want to hear about them. The truth is that Hemingway, Ruth and Rose—and let's add General George Patton here—had special gifts along with major flaws in their characters. Adulated, placed on pedestals, they chose not to deal with their character defects. (Rose still has time to do so since he has gone for treatment). This makes them memorable personalities, but not strong men. God would probably see them as incomplete men, not having lived up to their potential.

These men and countless millions more develop their physical skills, and often their mental attributes, but fall short in the spiritual dimension. They label this third area "religion" and for a hundred reasons decide it's not for them.

What they're saying may go something like this: "I don't need You, God. I've done pretty well on my own."

Yes, they have, but only until life hands them a challenge they can't handle on their own.

Who are the truly strong men?

Starting with men of the Bible, here's a list of six of the strongest:

Abraham
Joseph
Moses

David

Peter

Paul

As I look at this list I am struck immediately by something they all had in common—a glaring weakness in the make-up of each one.

Abraham—too cowardly to tell the truth that lovely Sarah was his wife. He feared the Egyptian king would want him out of the way. "Tell him you're my sister," he instructed her weakly. This was partly true because she was his half-sister, but an escape route nonetheless.

Joseph—so arrogant, self-righteous and insensitive toward his brothers that they wanted to kill him.

Moses—so lacking in courage and self-worth that he refused to accept the leadership role God offered him. "Get my brother Aaron to do it," he whined.

David—so self-centered he broke most of the Ten Commandments, including adultery and murder.

Peter—a loud-mouthed buffoon who denied Jesus three times.

Paul—such an all-out legalist, so hardhearted, he was zealous in his persecution of the Church, starting with his endorsement of the stoning of Stephen.

On the surface not a very promising lot. Weakness became strength, however, when the Spirit of God made each one of them strong in their weak places.

The twelve men Christ chose to work with had little strength on their own. When Christ was captured through the betrayal of one of them—who hanged himself afterward—they all fled, saying, in effect, as Peter did, "I don't want to be identified with that Man Jesus."

What changed them?

The falling of the Spirit of God on them and other followers in the Upper Room at Pentecost.

Even though the disciples had been devoted followers of Jesus for three years, this new spiritual infusion was necessary before they could go out boldly and enthusiastically as strong males to minister to a sick world.

Only the breath of God could have turned that weak husband, Abraham, into the Father of a nation.

Only His Spirit could have used self-centered Joseph to save an empire from starvation, then filled him with the compassion to forgive those who had wronged him.

Only God's Spirit could have transformed timid Moses into the great liberator of his people.

Only He could have made guilty David into the king whose reign was ever afterward remembered as the golden age of Law.

Only the Spirit could have turned traitorous Peter into the fearless leader and martyr of the early Church.

Only the breath of God could have changed the arrogant, merciless persecutor of Christians, Saul, into Paul, the courageous, indefatigable evangelist of the Good News.

Thawing the Inner Man

Clive Staples Lewis, one of the great intellects and authors of this century, was for years the complete boss of his life. Knowing somehow that God was a threat to his desire to be in control, he became an atheist.

As he put it in his book *Surprised by Joy*, "I had always wanted, above all things, not to be 'interfered with.' I had wanted (mad wish) 'to call my soul my own.' I had been far more anxious to avoid suffering than to achieve delight. My ideal of virtue would never be allowed to lead me into anything intolerably painful; I would be 'reasonable.' "

Yet C. S. Lewis did not find any joy and fulfillment as a frozen male in that little world of his. He became restless, began searching. A change took place gradually in his mind and heart. The key turning point in his thawing took place on a bus when he suddenly admitted to himself the growing conviction of the reality of God. "It seemed like I was wearing some stiff clothing, like a suit of armor. . . . I felt myself being given a free choice. I could unbuckle the armor or keep it on. I chose to unbuckle. . . . Then came the repercussion on the imaginative level. I felt as if I were a man of snow at long last beginning to melt. The melting was starting in my back—drip-drip . . . trickle-trickle."

The problem of letting go his ego and pride was enormous. As Lewis put it, "When finally I gave in and admitted God was God, I was perhaps the most reluctant convert in all England."

Loosed from his intellectual frozenness, C. S. Lewis went on to write some 25 books that have been stepping-stones to faith for millions of people, one of which, *Mere Christianity*, was a key factor in turning around the life of Charles Colson, famous for his role as "hatchet-man" in the administration of Richard Nixon.

A former Marine, Colson prided himself on his macho role in getting things done for the President. He did his job so well he incurred the antagonism of most of Washington, and later became one of the Watergate men sentenced to prison terms.

Some months before his conviction and sentence a story

had circulated about Colson that most of Washington scoffed at—that Chuck had gone through some kind of religious experience.

"Phony as a three-dollar bill," was one reporter's reaction.

Yet the reports persisted that the Nixon hatchet-man was involved in a prayer group and, yes, *was different*. I was asked one day if I would be willing to see Colson in prison and advise him about writing a book.

I did so with reservations; like many others I was somewhat skeptical of the validity of his conversion. When Chuck came to Washington, under guard, to testify in the Watergate hearings, I met with him in an adjoining room. We sparred with words for a while, then he suggested we pray together. As I listened to Chuck talk to the Lord with simplicity and sincerity, my doubts dissolved. When he was released from prison a few months later, together we began working on a manuscript for Chosen Books that became *Born Again*. In it he described his thawing experience.

It happened one night when Chuck visited his businessman friend Tom Phillips. Phillips had given Colson a copy of C. S. Lewis' *Mere Christianity*. That night they went over the part about pride, including these paragraphs:

There is one vice of which no man in the world is free; which everyone in the world loathes when he sees it in someone else; there is no fault which we are more unconscious of in ourselves—I'm talking about pride.

Pride has been the chief cause of misery in every nation and in every family since the world began. A proud man is always looking down on things and people. And of course as long as you are looking down you cannot see something that is above you.

Chuck had come to Phillips' home feeling a deep restlessness in his spirit. These words pierced him.

"I felt naked and unclean, my bravado defenses gone," Colson wrote in *Born Again.* "I was exposed, unprotected, for Lewis' words were describing me. One passage in particular seemed to sum up what had happened to all of us at the White House:

> For pride is spiritual cancer: it eats up the very possibility of love, or contentment, or even common sense.

Tom Phillips asked Chuck about his relationship with God. Chuck admitted he had none. Then Tom suggested that they pray together. Chuck nodded and wrote later that "as Tom prayed, something began to flow into me—a kind of energy. Then came a wave of emotion which nearly brought tears. I fought them back."

When Chuck said good-bye and drove out of Tom's driveway, the tears started. He pulled to the side of the road, leaned his head against the wheel. "I forgot about machismo," he wrote. "I forgot about pretenses, about fears of being weak. And as I did, I began to experience a wonderful feeling of being released. There came the strange sensation that water was not only running down my cheeks, but surging through my whole body as well, cleansing and cooling as it went."

And then Chuck prayed his first prayer: "God, I don't

know how to find You, but I'm going to try! I'm not much the way I am now, but somehow I want to give myself to You."

Following his thawing-out experience—or melting, as Lewis called it—Chuck became a part of a closely knit fellowship of men who studied Scripture, prayed and fellowshiped together. *Born Again* made a huge impact on America, sold in the millions and enabled Chuck to launch his Prison Fellowship ministry, which has redeemed and restored to usefulness thousands of former inmates.

The Strength to Change

The strong men of today have, by a decision of their wills, torn off their protective coverings, shed the masks and taken a close look at the persons inside. Where they saw shallowness and phoniness, they took the painful steps toward change. Many of them had not wanted to change. They felt they had already discovered their true selves when they abandoned moral standards and joined the sexual revolution. With that revolution a failure, once again they had to start a search for their true identities.

Kirk Douglas, who has played gutsy roles in films for many years, put it this way: "Men are learning to be strong enough to show softness, hurt, anxiety, doubt, fear—all of which men have to live with from time to time."

Richard Roundtree, who played the tough-guy role in the "Shaft" movies, put it even more bluntly: "Being male in this country has been a burden and a bore. But the concept is changing. We men no longer need to pretend to be what we are not. I'm a combination of traits: sometimes strong, other times shy. I'm fearless and yet fearful. I'm a tiger and I'm a pussycat. I'm a whole human being with a full range of emotions and that makes me feel alive."

It has become more and more obvious that the stereotyped male—rugged, aggressive, ruthless—usually does a poor job with all his relationships.

In *Male Chauvinism*, Michael Korda depicts with devastating candor how men have attempted to be strong by suppressing women: "It was clearly not a result of ruthless strength and selfishness on the part of men, but the sign of their inner weakness, fear, and frustration. . . . The male chauvinist is not the proud figure that men take him to be, insisting on his legitimate superiority over women, but rather a man who cannot accept the responsibility for the failures of his life and therefore assigns them to women."

The women's liberation movement has been the inevitable result of all the male put-downs of women. Concerned with legitimate grievances over unfair practices in the working world, "women's libbers" won wide support among both sexes.

Some men, perhaps feeling guilty over their chauvinism, or eager to claim their liberation, have started encounter groups to renounce machismo, putting up signs like "Boycott *Playboy*" . . . "End compulsive 'maskulinity.' " A newspaper named *Brother* has called for reexamination of men's roles as sex symbols. Some of the points:

- We men are often exploited as sex objects.
- We are oppressed by the limitations on our sensuality and compassion.
- There is an abridgment of our freedom to self-

determine our sexuality and be expressive with other men.

Though some of this may be a rationale for homosexuality, there are legitimate questions here for men to look at. Have we trained ourselves to be cold and unfeeling? Are we so afraid of being called a "queer" that we shun any expression of warmth and affection toward other men? Are we, as one man wrote, "haunted, taunted men, bombarded by images of what we are not: studs, athletes, intellectuals, leaders, fighters"?

Men and Babies

One beautiful expression of the compassionate male is the "Men Who Love Babies" program at St. Luke's-Roosevelt Hospital Center in New York City.

Bill Gale is one of more than a hundred men who volunteer to cuddle, talk to, feed and diaper babies, most born of drug-addicted mothers and thus with no fit home to go to. They're known as "boarder babies."

"There is an emergence through this program of the new, sensitized man," reports Bill Gale. "The uncovered myth is that men relate more to objects, while women are more sensitive to people. Not true of the baby-holders I know."

Ian McCart, 43, a banker and a bachelor, got hooked on these babies. "I love to sit quietly with a baby and listen to classical music on the nursery radio. It's soothing for both of us, and usually the first peace I have all day long."

The men have their specialties with the babies. Bill loves to rub heads, moving his fingers in a slow, circular fashion until he gets a tiny, gummy smile. Steve is a back-patter. Ed sings to them. Kevin rubs noses with them.

It's a two-way ministry, the report in *Parade* magazine continues. The men do a deep healing work with traumatized infants. In return, they find themselves becoming more fully human.

How sad that some men feel they are strong when they decide they will make it on their own without any help from God, thank you! Since God gave all His children freedom to accept or reject Him, it grieves me when I see men nursing their anger and hatred of God until death. What do they think will happen to them then? That eternal oblivion will somehow free them from their bitterness?

Sometimes I get cold chills when I contemplate what might have happened to me if I had not let Him into my life.

When I rebelled from my Christian upbringing and turned my back on both God and His Son, I began a fifteen-year trek into the wilderness. The inner freezing process began. Each time I broke away from moral restraints implanted in my childhood, something hardened inside of me.

Yet God did not turn His back on me. He was with me when I was farthest from Him. Once a group of us pilots were at the Officers Club in the early morning hours after a long poker game. Alcohol flowed freely. Suddenly, I heard these words coming out of my mouth: "I don't know what it is, but after the war I'm supposed to do something important in this world."

"Sure you are, Torchy. I see you running a casino at Las Vegas."

I shook my head. "No, more creative than that. Write a

book, perhaps. Be a missionary, even. I don't know. It's just something I feel inside me."

The next day when we all had sobered up, my buddies kidded me. "You were really flying high last night, Torchy. If you ever become a missionary, you can come and get us all straightened out."

I was embarrassed, wondering whence those words I spoke the night before had sprung. About the last thing I ever wanted to be, I thought, was anything religious.

When the war ended, I bought a secondhand automobile with my poker winnings and in January 1946 headed back toward Texas with everything I owned in the trunk of my car (clothes, typewriter, golf clubs). I would look up my flying buddies and begin writing the great American novel about returning servicemen.

It didn't happen, of course. I returned to my home near Boston and thought about starting a sports magazine. Instead, in 1946, I found myself in New York working as a reporter at *Guideposts*, a religious publication.

What a strange turn! The only reason I went to that young adult meeting at the Marble Collegiate Church a few months later was because I was told it was a great place to meet young, attractive single women.

And then came my thawing that weekend at Ramapo, New York.

Today as I look back over my life, everything good that has happened to me stems from the transaction I made that Saturday night—a transfer of control of my life to God almighty.

As a man did I suddenly become stronger?

Definitely yes.

How?

Before Ramapo I had tight control over the way I lived my life. I had the freedom to do what I wanted to do when I wanted to do it. Outside forces exerted pressure on me to some extent, but at any point I could say, "The hell with it," and move on to something else.

The trouble with this—I was miserable. I didn't like myself. I had tunnel vision. My life was shallow, meaningless. I had placed myself on the throne as god of my life. As a result, I was defenseless against the subtle forces of darkness. This is bondage; this is weakness.

Reaching out to a Higher Power changed the direction of my life. I was no longer alone on an island of self. By admitting my insufficiency, I was freed from the impossible task of always having to be right . . . and then when I wasn't, falling into the abyss of self-doubt, self-pity, self-repudiation.

Looking to God for strength suddenly took the pressure off of me. Being dependent wasn't weakness, it was reality. For I was dependent. I had no control over life—or death. Someone else created me, brought me into the world as a helpless baby. As much as I might rail against it, the day would come when I would leave this world just as I had entered it—not in control.

Strength came in accepting all this. Strength came in knowing that whereas I was weak, my God in heaven was strong. His strength would overcome my weakness. Seeing this pumped life into my spirit. I felt a new stirring in my creativity.

I was stronger now in another way, too. The support of new friends; they seemed more than friends, teammates in a cause, people I could call for support at times of need.

Setbacks were ahead. Times of doubt and discouragement. But on this new walk I sensed I would get stronger. The strength was not something I had to generate; it would come from outside of myself. Along the way, "I take pleasure in infirmities, . . . in persecutions, in distresses for Christ's sake: for when I am weak, then am I strong."

Questions for Reflection

1) What is your definition of a strong man?
2) Whom do you consider to be the strongest man living today? What is the basis of his strength?
3) Would he have been your choice as the strongest man ten years ago? Explain.
4) Knowing that every man has both a feminine and masculine element inside him, how does this affect your relationship with male friends?
5) What did Paul mean when he said, "When I am weak, then am I strong"?

14
Behold, the Man!

Then came Jesus forth. . . .

John 19:5, KJV

Some years ago ten people at a dinner party began to discuss a movie about Jesus Christ. It led to an intense sharing of different feelings and opinions about the movie and the Man. The attractive young woman seated next to me, however, was bored by the subject. "Why would anyone want to be like Jesus?" she asked.

A long silence followed, then the conversation veered to another subject. Yet I found myself fascinated by that silence. What thoughts, unexpressed, filled the minds of the ten of us?

Three of us were strong believers in His deity. Why had we remained silent? Were we reluctant to take a stand on our convictions? Fearful perhaps that we would appear pious?

Three others, from what they said, accepted Christ as a historical person, but seemed embarrassed to talk about Him. Respectable churchgoers, you might call them, struggling with their beliefs.

Two of the dinner guests were openly hostile, resenting "those fanatical Bible spouters, always pushing their beliefs on other people." They rejected any claim to a unique position for Jesus.

The bored young woman and her husband were not interested in the discussion at all.

In thinking about this episode later, I realized that our various attitudes toward Jesus were a microcosm of the whole world. Our beliefs ranged from rejection to indifference to acceptance to discipleship.

It is Jesus, the Man, who has caused such controversy for the past 2,000 years. People can accept or reject God in a fairly clean-cut manner. They either believe in a Creator or they don't, but not with the intensity of feelings that surround His Son.

These facts about Jesus are often quoted:

He was born in an obscure village called Bethlehem.

His mother was a teenager, a peasant girl.

He grew up in another village, Nazareth.

He worked as a carpenter until He was thirty.

For three years He moved about the land as an itinerant preacher.

He never married.

He never wrote a book.

He never held office.

He never owned a home.

He never traveled more than 200 miles from the place where He was born.

And yet this one Man has impacted our world like no other man.

I can relate to every person at that dinner party, because at some period of my life I have been where they were. I have gone through five stages in my relationship with Jesus. I have known five Christs. Readers of this book will, I am sure, identify at some point with my journey.

1. Meek, Gentle Jesus

As a boy I met Jesus for the first time at my Sunday school class. His picture was on the wall. I thought He was a strange-looking man: a lot of hair, clothes that didn't fit too well, sandals (no one wore sandals in our town). He also looked anemic.

My Sunday school teacher was an unattractive woman who talked about the meekness of this "gentle Jesus," who died on the cross for our sins. I couldn't understand this at all. I didn't have any sins that I knew of—if I did, no one had bothered to point them out to me. Of course, I got spanked every now and then for doing things like throwing stones at a car, telling lies and disobeying my parents, but if these were sins nobody said so.

No, this Sunday school Jesus was not very impressive. He didn't play ball, He didn't have much of a job and a lot of people got angry at Him.

My father was a pastor until I was six years old. He was a gentle man, like Jesus, I thought, but my father had played baseball in college so was much more of a man. When Dad decided he didn't want to be a preacher but a professor, I concluded that religion wasn't very important. This had to be true of Jesus, too, so I dismissed Him from my mind. The men I admired were athletes, explorers, people like Charles Lindbergh.

2. The Historical Christ

When I enrolled at Ohio Wesleyan University, I discovered to my annoyance that I was required to take a Bible course in my freshman year. Though the teaching was pretty dull, I was forced to study the Bible. In the process I discovered the historical Jesus.

He really did live on this earth! I dismissed the virgin birth theory, as did others in the class, but the documentation of this Man's life was indisputable.

Furthermore, seeing Christ in the historical perspective was a comfortable position for me to take toward Him. The historical Jesus is set far back from the stream of life.

With this approach, one is not likely to be shunned or considered a fanatic for his beliefs. He can join the intellectual chorus and recite that, "Jesus was a good man. He had some good advice for us, but let's be realistic about those myths and fairy tales in the Bible."

In my case, putting Christ in this setting was a simple solution during college and military service years. The historical Jesus did not interfere with anything I wanted to do.

True, faced with the cold, clammy fear of death during the war, I desperately needed a philosophy. The historical Christ was too remote to be of any help. And so I settled on an attitude of nonchalance, which meant that nothing was really important, not even life itself.

3. Christ, the Teacher

My drift from this "historical" relationship with Christ to a considerably closer one began in 1946. I had been out of the Air Corps for a year, wandering around the country collecting material to write a novel. But the novel did not materialize; my philosophy of nonchalance left me unfit to face the competition and realities of the post-war world.

A spiritual change began to take place inside me when as a reporter for *Guideposts* I interviewed people of achievement who had at the core of their lives a strong faith. Time and again what had guided their successful personal and career decisions were the teachings of Jesus.

This was a new Jesus to me. A Man who was always confounding His critics, puncturing the balloons of the pompous, refusing to conform to what He saw as dull, impractical religious practices.

"You shall walk only so far on the Sabbath," the scribes and Pharisees taught.

Jesus walked as far as was necessary.

"Certain things you may eat and other things you shall not eat," these religious teachers ordered.

"You're not defiled by what goes into your mouth," Jesus answered, "but by what comes out."

I liked the way Christ bucked the sanctimonious religious leaders of that time, was intrigued by His strategy for selecting His disciples. He didn't conduct a series of interviews of top prospects in the business community. He didn't post a notice about His intentions. He went about His business of meeting people where they lived.

Passing along the shores of a lake one day, He saw two fishermen busy with their nets. To have broken in on them with an offer of employment as preachers of a new religion would have invited a quick rebuff. Jesus had a different approach.

"Come with Me," He said, "and I will make you fishers of men."

Fishers—that was a word they could understand. Fishers of men—it sounded interesting. . . . Let's hear what the Man has to say.

Later He sat on a hillside to teach a group of people, most of whom were farmers. "A sower went forth to sow," Jesus began, "and when he sowed some seeds fell by the wayside and the fowls came and devoured them up. . . ."

Were the farmers interested? Every man of them had gone through that experience! The thievish crows—many a good day's work they had spoiled. This Teacher knew something about their troubles. We want to hear more. . . .

Then there was His encounter with the Samaritan woman at the well. Because of the animosity between Samaritans and Jews, the woman at first must have resented Jesus' being there. So Jesus didn't confront her, but spoke quietly, musingly, as if to Himself.

"If you knew who I am," He said, "you would ask and I would give you living water."

The woman stopped short, her interest challenged in spite of herself.

"What are You talking about? Are You greater than our father Jacob who gave us this well? Have You some magic that will save us this long walk in the sun?"

With sure instincts Jesus began to talk to her in terms of her own life, her ambitions, her hopes. When the disciples came up a few minutes later, they found the unbelievable—a Samaritan woman listening with rapt attention to the teaching of a Jew.

As I studied Christ's teaching techniques, I found myself applying them to my own life:

Ask, and it shall be given you; seek and you will find . . . helpful advice for an ambitious young man.

I can do all things through Christ who strengthens me . . . a guideline for overcoming my phobia about public speaking.

I was learning and growing. It took me some time, however, to see the selfishness of my approach—*that I was now interested in Jesus Christ not for what and who He was, but only for what He could do for me.*

4. Christ, the Man

My church fellowship with the young adult group nudged me into my fourth relationship with Jesus—where I encountered Christ, the Man.

The change in me began when I was asked to do a book review on *The Man Nobody Knows* by Bruce Barton, of Barton, Barton, Durstine and Osborne advertising firm. Reading this book and reporting on it to people of my own age changed my concept of Jesus yet again.

Right at the start Bruce Barton debunked the idea that Jesus was weak and effeminate. Instead, Barton portrayed Him in the carpentry shop, His body lean from a disciplined life, His muscles strong from hard work. "Jesus learned to fell trees in the forest and shape them with an adz," Barton wrote. "Often He was seen trudging into the woods with His ax over His shoulder, returning at nightfall with a rough-hewn beam."

The young Jesus "waxed strong," as Scripture tells us, taking long walks across a rugged terrain. Rigorous self-discipline prepared Him for that forty-day fast He endured at the start of His ministry, during which time He touched no food. Satan tested Jesus three times, once urging Him to turn stones into bread. Jesus could have done it. His flesh must have been terribly tempted.

The youth who had been a carpenter stayed in the wilderness forty days; a man came out. Men who looked on Him from that hour felt the authority of one who has put his physical and spiritual house in order.

The testing time in the desert helped give Jesus the inner fortitude He needed to face hardship, fatigue, opposition. It prepared Him for that day He entered the Jerusalem Temple, described vividly by Bruce Barton:

> The air was filthy with the smell of animals and human beings herded together. Hard-faced priests and money-changers sat behind long tables, exacting the utmost farthing from those who came to buy.
>
> As Jesus faced the sordid reality, His cheeks flushed. Suddenly He strode to the table where the fat money-changer sat, and hurled it violently across the court. He charged onward. He reached the counters where the dove cages stood; with quick, sure movements the cages were opened and the occupants released. Brushing aside the dealers in front of the cattle pens, He threw down the bars and drove the bellowing animals out into the streets.
>
> Jesus stood flushed and panting, His eyes sweeping scornfully over the faces distorted by anger and greed. "This is my authority," He cried. "It is written, 'My house shall be called a house of prayer for all the nations,' but ye have made it a den of robbers."

Seeing Christ as an outdoor man, a confrontative, courageous man, was extremely important in my Christian walk. Now I could better understand why the men of His time were drawn to Him. And now I was ready for a closer relationship with Him myself.

Christ the Man was no longer the anemic figure on the Sunday school wall. No longer a remote, historical figure. He was much more than a great Teacher. He was alive to me, a Friend I talked and prayed to, a real Person. My life had turned around.

What more did I need?

Always something more, I was to discover. Always growth. If faith isn't growing, then it's declining.

Strong as my faith was becoming, I was not spiritually undergirded for the calamity in my personal life that came ten years after my personal experience with the Man Jesus. The breakup of a marriage is devastating. The question I asked then was "Why?"

I had given my life to Christ, had worked hard at being a good Christian. Behind my question was the feeling that all this Christian effort somehow should have made me immune from a personal disaster.

In the period of discouragement that followed, I came face to face with the spirit of evil. Never again will I think of the devil as a comical red-robed figure with a pitchfork. He is subtle and one of his most potent and persuasive tools for the conquest of a human being is self-pity.

When one is falling, the instinct is to reach out for something to hold on to. I did this and found one handle to clutch—my commitment experience kneeling at an altar ten years before. This was still very real to me. And so I knelt once more and sought Him again.

With this act of submission came a new recognition and acceptance of my frailty. And at this time of suffering and defeat in my own life, I saw, too, the weakness of Christ.

247

I saw Him dragged onto a balcony before a jeering crowd—slapped, whipped, blood running into His eyes from the thorns that circled His head. I heard the words of Pilate, words of a cynical Roman without a hint that all of history hinged on the events of that day. Words that have echoed through the ages with a meaning he never gave them:

"Behold, the Man!" (John 19:5).

Rejected by His fellow Jews, abandoned by His friends, Jesus was led out of the city to the agony of crucifixion. He endured the inhumanity of the Roman soldiers who drove the nails through His wrists, the scorn of bystanders who shouted obscenities at Him as He hung helplessly in the sun, flies already gathering on His naked body.

"Behold, the Man!"

5. The Indwelling Christ

As a man Jesus accepted the role of weakness assigned to Him. When He hung on the cross, He took on the sins of all mankind, a staggering collection of weaknesses. To Christ's disciples and followers, His death represented total defeat and failure.

Then, incredible good news!

Jesus did not remain in His tomb, defeated and dismissed as a fraud. He arose, ascended to heaven to assume His rightful position of strength beside His Father. But His mission was not yet completed. He returned to earth, gathered together His joyful disciples and told them, "You shall receive power when the Holy Spirit has come upon you."

The disciples then gathered in the Upper Room and prayed for many hours. The Bible describes the "rush of mighty wind" that came, and how "they were all filled with the Holy Spirit." What a sight this must have been! How indescribable the joy, the elation, the resurgence of power as these weak men were reborn! They were empowered to go forth and minister to the whole world, to show an utterly new strength and courage in the face of ridicule, beatings, imprisonment and execution.

In my fifth relationship with Jesus I have discovered that this same power is indeed available to us today.

When I asked the Spirit of Jesus to indwell me, to fill me, He accepted my invitation. Immediately there was a new joy, new energy and a new capacity to love others. As a man I looked the same on the outside, but on the inside I was different. With new clarity I saw that I would always be limited with what I could accomplish on my own strength. My weakness will always get me in trouble unless I lie my life on the altar every day and ask this indwelling Holy Spirit to provide the wisdom and the discernment and the vitality I need.

Strong men—weak men. We males are born with the inner ingredients to be either or both. The choice is ours. Deep down, of course, we want to be strong. But what makes the strong men of today? Who are they?

Money gives a man the power to control others, but in itself money does not make a man strong.

Athletic skill wins the adulation of others, but so often today these "heroes" have feet of clay.

Political leaders learn the art of compromise, a trait that too often weakens them.

Do we receive some guidelines as we look at the greatest Man who ever lived, the Man who, the ages have confirmed, was God Himself?

Above all, He came to be the servant of all.

The strong man, Christ teaches us, will take unpopular positions on issues he believes in, then he acts boldly, knowing that mighty forces will come to his support. He readily admits his mistakes, is quick to praise an opponent, holds back any judgment. A strong man has a rock-like patience; he is not deterred by criticism, but examines it prayerfully to see if he can learn from it.

The strong man will be celibate when this is called for; as a son he honors his parents; he is a faithful husband, a father who would not only lay down his life for his wife and children, but also give them the time they need; the strong man is a caring brother; he seeks the Lord's guidance in his work; he leads others by serving them; when he goes to church, he seeks ways to minister to others. He has a tender heart for the weak.

The strong man knows his Creator, joyfully accepts the way he was made, delights in the special skills he has been given and learns to use them for the good of mankind.

Most important, we men who seek to be strong know it will never happen through our own power—only through His.

Questions for Reflection

1) What is your relationship right now with Jesus?
2) Is the thought of being weak unacceptable to you?
3) Can you see strength coming out of your weakness?
4) Is the Holy Spirit real to you? In what way?
5) Assuming that you have invited Christ to indwell you, is there a next step for you to take? If so, what is it?

Bibliography

Barton, Bruce. *The Man Nobody Knows*. Indianapolis: Bobbs-Merrill, 1925.

Botwin, Carol. *Men Who Can't Be Faithful*. New York: Warner Books, 1988.

Bradford, Brick; Leonard E. LeSourd; Betty Schonauer; Rev. William P. Showalter; Rev. Robert C. Whitaker. *Healing for the Homosexual*. Oklahoma City: Presbyterian Reformed and Renewal Ministries, 1978.

Brothers, Dr. Joyce. *What Every Woman Should Know About Men*. New York: Simon and Schuster, 1981.

Casale, Anthony M., and Philip Lerman. *USA Today: Tracking Tomorrow's Trends*. Kansas City, N.Y.: Andrews, McMeel and Parker, 1986.

Cole, Edwin Louis. *Maximized Manhood*. Springdale Penn.: Whitaker House, 1982.

Dalbey, Gordon. *Healing the Masculine Soul*. Waco: Word Books, 1944.

Dobson, Dr. James C. *Straight Talk to Men and Their Wives.* Waco: Word Books, 1980.

Dubbert, Joe L. *A Man's Place.* Englewood Cliffs, N.J.: Prentice-Hall, Inc. 1979.

Farrell, Warren, Ph.D. *Why Men Are the Way They Are.* New York: Berkley Books, 1986.

Forward, Dr. Susan and Joan Torres. *Men Who Hate Women and the Women Who Love Them.* New York: Bantam Books, 1987.

Getz, Gene A. *The Measure of a Man.* Ventura, Calif.: Regal Books, 1974.

Gilder, George. *Naked Nomads (Unmarried Men in America).* New York: Quadrangle/The New York Times Book Co., 1974.

Goldberg, Herb. *The New Male.* New York: William Morrow & Company, 1979.

Grossvogel, David I. *Dear Ann Landers.* New York: Berkley Books, 1987.

Jeffers, Susan, Ph.D. *Opening Our Hearts to Men.* New York: Fawcett Columbine, 1989.

Kiley, Dr. Dan. *The Peter Pan Syndrome (Men Who Have Never Grown Up).* New York: Dodd, Mead & Company, 1983.

Kilgore, James E. *The Intimate Man.* Nashville: Abingdon Press, 1984.

Korda, Michael. *Male Chauvinism!* New York: Berkley Publishing Corporation, 1972, 1973.

Lawrence, Brother. *The Practice of the Presence of God.* Old Tappan, N.J.: Fleming H. Revell Company.

Levinson, Daniel J. *The Seasons of a Man's Life.* New York: Ballantine Books, 1978.

Lewis, Clive Staples. *Surprised by Joy.* New York: Harcourt, Brace and Jovanovich, Inc., 1956.

Mornell, Pierre, M.D. *Passive Men, Wild Women.* New York: Ballantine Books, 1979.

Payne, Leanne. *Crisis in Masculinity.* Westchester, Ill.: Crossway Books, 1985.

Petersen, J. Allan. *For Men Only.* Wheaton, Ill.: Tyndale House Publishers, 1973.

Roper, David. *The Strength of a Man.* Grand Rapids, Mich.: Discovery House, 1973.

Rosin, Bruce. *Stepfathering.* New York: Simon and Schuster, 1987.

Smith, F. Lagard. *Men of Strength for Women of God.* Eugene, Ore.: Harvest House Publishers, 1989.

Stanley, Charles F. *A Man's Touch.* Wheaton, Ill.: Victor Books, Division of Scripture Press Publications, 1977.

Walker, James. *Husbands Who Won't Lead and Wives Who Won't Follow.* Minneapolis: Bethany House, 1989.

Wideman, John Edgar. *Brothers and Keepers.* New York: Holt, Rinehart and Winston, 1984.